STACEY COLE'S NEW HAMPSHIRE

STACEY COLE'S
NEW HAMPSHIRE

A Lyrical Landscape

Stacey Cole

ILLUSTRATIONS BY DEBORAH ANDERSEN

PLAIDSWEDE PUBLISHING
Concord, New Hampshire

Designed and composed in Adobe Garamond Premier Pro at Hobblebush Books, Brookline, New Hampshire (www.hobblebush.com)

Printed in the United States of America

ISBN 978-0-9889176-6-8
Library of Congress Control Number: 2013956031

Published by:

PLAIDSWEDE PUBLISHING
P.O. Box 269 · Concord, New Hampshire 03302-0269
www.plaidswede.com

For my readers

ACKNOWLEDGMENTS

I have been so fortunate to have had a great deal of help and encouragement in writing these "Nature Talks" columns. This book is dedicated to our readers, for without their loyalty there would have been no column.

I wish to sincerely thank "others," so to speak, who work behind the scene. These folks also have really cared about the "Nature Talks" column and greatly contributed to its having lasted into its 52nd year of publication in the *Union Leader*.

Bill and Nackey Loeb were the first to encourage me to write and I doubt they missed reading many columns.

Joe McQuaid, current president and publisher of the *Union Leader*, has greatly encouraged me to continue writing. I specially thank Joe for his kind words that appear on the back cover.

Thanks to my very good friend of many years, former New Hampshire Governor Stephen Merrill, for the kinds words which he contributed especially for this book's back cover.

Throughout the years, there have been editorial page editors who have checked my writing to make sure it was grammatically and generally correct. In 1962, the year I began writing, T.A. Dearborn set up the column and guided it carefully. John Hammons succeeded him and both told me they enjoyed doing so, as did Jim Finnegan when he took over from John. In recent years Jim Ferriter has been watching the column closely for any mistakes. These gentlemen became good friends to me, and my writing was improved because of their good work.

In the early years, my late wife Mildred and our good friend, the late Becky Brusie, assisted with the column. Becky did the typing, and both suggested subject matter.

Early in 1966, I retired after 25 years of commercial farming to become the executive director of the New Hampshire Petroleum Council, a subsidiary of the American Petroleum Institute. Arlene Potter Mosher, was my executive assistant and typed and edited the column. With her long editorial experience, I knew that my errors would be corrected before the column was forwarded to the *Union Leader*. After Arlene's retirement, Virgina Bigwood, took over the task in exemplary fashion. Thanks to both.

Many thanks to Dr. Bonnie Breen-Wagner, professor emerita of English at Plymouth State University, for writing the introduction to this book. Also to Deborah Andersen, BFA at Plymouth State University, for her splendid artwork on the front cover and inside the book.

A special thank-you to Mr. George Geers of Plaidswede Publishing who believed that my writing should again receive the light of day in the form of this and possibly a future book.

—Stacey Cole

Contents

Introduction

"Several of nature's people
I know, and they know me;
I feel for them a transport
Of cordiality."
—Emily Dickinson

IN 2003, Plymouth State University honored Stacey W. Cole with the Robert Frost Contemporary American Award, named for America's late poet laureate who taught at Plymouth in the early 20th century. The award recognizes "those individuals whose service to the people of New England best exemplifies Frost's values of hard work, humanitar ianism, and devotion to the country 'north of Boston.'"

Stacey Cole epitomizes the specifics of this prestigious award. Born in Keene, New Hampshire in 1921, Stacey has devoted himself to the state of New Hampshire and its citizens in countless ways which made him the ideal choice to join the select group of Frost award recipients, among them the late former Governor Walter Peterson, Pulitzer Prize-winning poet Maxine Kumin, and former U.S. Senator Norris Cotton. A graduate of what is now the Thompson School of Applied Science and the man for whom the University of New Hampshire's Cole Hall is named, Stacey's many accomplishments include serving in the N.H. House of Representatives (three years as deputy speaker); president of the

N.H. Farm Bureau Federation (the youngest ever elected in the U.S.); first chairman of the N.H. Air Resources Commission; senior agricultural advisor to the American Petroleum Institute; executive director of the N.H. Petroleum Council; trustee of the University System of New Hampshire; moderator for the town of Swanzey, active representative for Governors Merrill and Shaheen on the N.H. Veterans Cemetery Committee, and many more too numerous to mention here, but all at the heart of doing for New Hampshire's citizens, especially its farmers.

Stacey, a farmer himself, has lived at Red Crow Farm in Swanzey, New Hampshire since 1941. He and his late wife, Mildred, actively farmed for 25 years, raising Jersey cattle and managing 5,000 laying hens. Indeed, Stacey and Mildred were married at midnight in their new henhouse with Mildred carrying one of her prized pullets as her bouquet. They enjoyed a one-day honeymoon in order to get back and care for their animals, a reminder of how much Stacey exemplifies devotion to the country north of Boston.

Of all Stacey's accomplishments, none renders him more dearly to New Hampshire citizens and readers across the country than his weekly newspaper column, "Nature Talks," now in its 52nd year of publication. Stacey's purpose in writing this column has always been to bring his readers' attention to this beautiful natural world God has provided all of us. My late mother was one such reader, a fine habit she passed on to me! For many years she read "Nature Talks" and wrote to Stacey with observations of various flora and fauna, and when she could, she would call and discuss these many things with him. Stacey's column and his calls were cherished opportunities to bring nature to her since she could not get about outside her home. In this busy workaday world, Stacey's column provides a refuge for readers, a few moments for reflection, a transport to the past, especially for those of us for whom Stacey's crisp, vivid images conjure up a quieter time we fondly recollect. Such a precious gift Stacey has for returning his mind to those times and sharing them with all of us in a "prose poetry" that entices us to return to his column week after week.

I have, for many years, wondered why no one has published Stacey's body of work to preserve forever his depictions of farm life, insights into animal behavior, ornithological observations, and New Hampshire ways of being. So many of us have learned so much from him as he researches our many queries and returns his answers in such vivid, imagistic writing. How fortunate for all of us that this collection of Stacey's essays has come to be!

—Bonnie Breen-Wagner
Professor Emerita, English
Plymouth State University
Plymouth, New Hampshire

AUTHOR'S NOTE

SINCE 1962, "Nature Talks from Down on the Farm" has appeared as a weekly feature on the pages of the *Manchester Union Leader* and now *New Hampshire Union Leader*.

My writing comes from my love of nature. I write about what I see. But I do not use my eyes only. I use all my senses. At times my observations are sprinkled with imagination, but those times are plain enough for all to see.

Over the years, I have been favored by receiving thousands of letters from my readers. Many of these contained a request that some day selections from these columns be put in a book.

So here they are, put together with deep appreciation. I hope the reading will give you pleasure. I enjoy writing "Nature Talks from Down on the Farm."

—Stacey Cole

STACEY COLE'S NEW HAMPSHIRE

I'd Like to Dip My Pen

I'D LIKE TO DIP MY PEN in the morning mist and write of whispering woods—of their soft sounds and quiet ways. I'd not even mind the scream of a jay, if it didn't repeat upon itself and call forth a cacophony that would break the spell. For spell it is when sounds are muted beyond their individual recognition.

I like a nothing background from time to time, so that my thoughts can be heard. It's like my very soul has taken nourishment from the surroundings and is endeavoring to communicate.

I walk over damp leaves which complain not at my passing. My eyes are soothed by the sight of straight lines of mists striking from sky to ground through lanes of trees. The lines of light seem to pass through branches as if they were nothing at all. But wait! Do the lines fall or rise?

I ponder.

If, indeed, they rise from spring-damp earth, seeking escape into Heaven, then I must look to that explanation.

Sometimes our eyes play tricks on us and we see what, in reality, is not there. Our minds jump to conclusions and lead us down wrong pathways. On further thought, maybe not wrong pathways. For what is right or wrong except by interpretation?

I see a squirrel on the trunk of a tree. He faces upward and my mind says he's climbing. A moment passes and he backs downward to inspect the underside of a bole. He was, in reality, descending.

Am I, therefore, forgiven for being wrong when I thought I was right?

The Shagbark

All books have to have a beginning. So do families and the places they live. I went Down on the Farm to live in the fall of 1941. But before I lived there (I was still single then), I looked the place over pretty good. I wanted to make sure that it was the place for me to make a beginning. This story, then, takes us back to those days, although it was written in April of '64.

THIS SPRING THE SHAGBARK on the hill will not waken. Its time to sleep has come. The old hickory stands almost at the top of the hill behind our barn and for many years it has been in a position to witness the farm's owners as they have come and gone.

Over a quarter century ago it watched me as I walked over the farm. Of course, I can only suppose it noticed me. Perhaps it had been engaged in more important matters and had not really taken note of a young man's passing. Being a sentimentalist, I like to imagine that the old tree did pay heed to what went on before it. Be that as it may, I noticed the old hickory. It was late summer and the great tree was handsome with its dark green leaves and wide-spreading boughs. It was a splendid tree, standing alone in a pasture.

That afternoon I was trying to decide whether this would be a good farm to work and to live on. I had been through the house and the attached sheds and had quickly appraised the old barn. I had walked the lines, followed the stone walls around the fields and had let them guide me through the woodlands. When I had had enough of walking, I sat down beneath the hickory and leaned back against its rough trunk. This was a welcome place, away from the hustle of the highway, and there was a coolness here out of the summer sun. I could see the whole farm and I looked at it well and for a long time. At last, beneath the old shagbark hickory, the decision was made. I would settle here.

Once the main decision had been made, my mind hurried on. I looked down upon the old barn, a square building in a state of dishevelment. Its large door was hanging from a single, twisted, rusty hinge. The roof had a gaping hole, the work of wind and rain and rotting rafters. I judged it had been built about the time of the American Revolution, for I was told the house dates back to the late 1700s.

Both the barn and the house were timbered with hand-hewn, old-growth pine. The marks of the adz that had been used to shape and roughly finish the joists and sills were plain to see. The builders used a jimmy-slick to cut and fit the mortises and tenons. The adz and the jimmy-stick are no longer used, but they served their time well. (I have one of each that have been in the Cole family for generations.)

The old barn was no longer of use and was torn down to make way for a modern poultry house. A great many changes have been demanded by the imposing years, some like new buildings for old and others that involved the land itself. The land where the hickory governed was of no value as pasture and white pine were allowed, yes, even encouraged to grow.

In the intervening years the pine have done well. However, like other crops, timber needs to be cultivated. I engaged a professional forester to weed out the hardwood and prune the straight pines so that they would put on inches of clear lumber. The large hickory was overtopping a number of good pines, pines that would yield well if freed from the shade and hunger of the hickory. The forester took his axe and opened several places in the bark of the tree and put 245T into the wounds. The deed was done—the hickory would sleep.

When I destroyed the old barn, a landmark was torn down. The change was progress. When the forester put the hickory to sleep, progress was again served.

I felt a twinge of sadness.

The Never-Failing Spring

A number of stories in this book have to do with the farm. I thought you'd best have a look at the place where you will be visiting within these pages. Many things you read about will take you through your imagination to faraway places in your memory, some perhaps long ago forgotten. That's all right, too, for these things could have happened anywhere. It is sort of like the mental pictures we used to draw of the people we listened to on the radio. Maybe when we saw their pictures they were a disappointment. Maybe not. But don't let that trouble you. Red Crow Farm to me is beautiful—as beautiful as you can imagine. So, welcome!

FOR AS LONG AS I CAN REMEMBER, I have heard the old adage, "You never miss the water 'til the well runs dry." Over the years we have been plagued with water troubles. When we first bought the farm, the old-timers said, "Well, there's one thing certain, you'll never have water trouble on the Bourne place." (That's what the folks in the village called our farm.) It was originally known as the Alcott place, having been built sometime in the late 1700s. Later it was called the Ball place, then the Bourne place. I never heard anyone refer to it as the Stickney place. Those were the folks we bought of. Now folks are beginning to refer to it as Red Crow Farm, even though we have only lived here a little over a third of a century, a modest amount of time to say the least.

The reason we were assured that we would never run out of water was because nobody ever had. Whenever the folks who lived here cleaned out the spring they had difficulty, for there was indeed a great flow of water. And it was good water, clear, bright and mighty tasty. It had a kind of sweet taste much as you might get out of an old lead pipe overflow.

Then one day, during a real dry spell, the spring failed. And when the rains came there was no recovery.

We dug a well up back of the henhouse where a dowser said to dig. Sure enough, we had a tremendous flow. But this didn't last either. When the frogs moved out, I asked the dowser what went wrong. He shrugged and replied, "The vein shifted."

We dug another hole next to the first and found the vein once more. We reset the pipes and the hens had good water. But not for long. The pipe soon ran aggravatingly slow and finally the trickle got down to a drip. And the hens went dry. Now an egg is mostly water and without the original intake the hen can't seem to do much except make smaller eggs. Unfortunately, the small egg market has never been a real snappy one. So we dug again. This time we found the vein on the other side of the first dig and once more reset the pipe.

Well, you guessed it. Another fine flow and then it lagged. Like a hired man we had once who would start out to the hayfield right spry but by noon was all dragged out.

This time we got hold of another dowser. He marched around holding onto his forked apple stick until suddenly it pointed downward, nearly breaking his wrists, so he reported. "Dig here," he said. "Twenty-one feet and you'll have all the water you'll ever need." This location was over 1,000 feet from the house and another 200 feet to the henhouse. But we needed the water and so we dug. This well turned out just as he said— "Twenty-one feet and plenty of water." It was a real tribute to the dowser profession. We were mighty pleased. That was in 1956 and by judicious use during dry times we did pretty well. Pretty well, that is, until 1971.

I hesitate to speak of it, but whenever the water runs dry there's another problem. Way back, someone had built a splendid little building back of the house. It was pine-paneled with marble steps leading to the door. The building itself was somewhat elevated and had a fine stone foundation. At some point in time another owner had installed modern facilities in the house and abandoned this useful structure. When we bought the place we found it in excellent repair and so I decided "Americana should be preserved." Time proved this to be one of my smarter days. (The marble steps were old gravestones that were brought to the farm by a former owner who was also the village sexton.)

But I have digressed.

When we ran out of water this time, my dad said, "Why don't you drill a well?" Now we had thought about this over the years but always rejected it. I don't know of a farmer who doesn't like his spring water. And I am no exception. However, there comes a time when "enough is enough," and so we now have a 310-foot well piped to the house and barn.

And may its waters ever flow—clear into the next century. If it does, the next few dry times won't be so bad, but they won't be so interesting either. And about that little building—I guess I'll keep it just in case.

Day's End (Early Summer)

AFTER THE "VESPER HOUR"—when evening becomes night and green hills have become black, shadowed forms—we say, "The day is done."

The cows are content in their stanchions, chewing their cuds. The calves sleep quietly in their pens, disturbed only lightly now and again by a pesky fly. The kittens, nestled close to one another, curled in tiny balls, await their mother's return with a morsel of mouse.

The barn is quiet, but down near the pond the night is loud with bubbling, round sounds and the middling high pitch in roundelay of frogs and toads. Mournfully repetitious, these deep night sounds are cut through from time to time with the high note of a single peeper, less energetic than in early spring and slower paced. The whining, distant bark of a village dog carries its cadence along with the repeated recitation of a whippoorwill.

Deepening darkness gradually stills the night.

Our Old Farm Truck

OUR OLD FARM TRUCK has acquired many voices during the past few years. It strikes up quite a melody as it travels along. It does very well on its own, but when it is carrying a part load of empty milk cans, the tunes become louder and more lively.

I am not often inclined to participate in this vocal disturbance but one bright morning late in May, when my spirits lifted me into

a rather carefree mood, I joined in the noisemaking. Without consulting either milk cans or truck, I selected the tune, "Down by the Old Mill Stream." The accompaniment was no worse than the soloist, but we had hardly accomplished the "eyes of blue" bit when we were interrupted by a small animal starting across the highway.

I slowed down abruptly, for it is never my intention to assist any animal into eternity if it can be helped. The milk cans protested vigorously as they banged against the truck cab. The old truck's brakes lent an eerie outcry as background to its general noise, but the little fellow proceeded safely on his way. To my amazement, I noted that it was a baby woodchuck, the smallest I had ever seen away from its mother. It either had become lost or was an orphan finding its own living.

Although he was traveling as fast as his tiny legs could carry him, his forward progress was slow. He was so tiny that for a moment I began to count on my fingers, much in the same manner as old Aunt Effie used to do after Town Meeting was over, while she studied the vital statistics section of the Town Report. The young woodchuck had either been born late, or he may not have grown too well. I had seen much larger baby woodchucks nibbling at the growing clover in our meadow within the past few days .

The last I saw of the little one, he was working himself into the stone wall that ran along the highway. At least he was safe for the moment.

Later that afternoon while planting corn by tractor, I saw another woodchuck. I had just turned my tractor around at the far end of the field and had started back planting the next two rows when I saw two crows and a woodchuck in positions that gave the impression they were visiting with one another.

At the tractor's approach, the crows finished their part of the conversation and departed for a large pine across the river. The woodchuck stood up on its hind legs, within four feet of the wheels, and watched me pass. He was still there on my return trip and again stood in salute. The next time my friend was no longer a spectator, for he had disappeared from view.

One thing a farmer early learns—as much as he may think so, he is never alone.

The Woodchuck

I CERTAINLY WAS SURPRISED the other day when Mildred said, "Look out the back window." And when I looked, I saw a woodchuck sitting beneath the lilac bushes. She'd been keeping a secret from me.

Now to see a woodchuck on the back lawn at the far edge would not be uncommon, but to see one beneath the lilacs which are right tight to the house struck me as rather strange. Before I could inquire further, Mildred informed me that he had a den under our woodpile.

Our back shed was built a great number of years ago, and there was some pretense at setting the building on stones. There was certainly no thought of cement work in those days and our woodpile rests upon the ground. In all the years we have been here, I haven't known a woodchuck to burrow under the edge of the building and take up an abode. Since this one is full grown, I suspect it is a male whose spouse has booted him out of the den, or he could be a single still searching for a mate.

Young woodchucks are born in early spring. Although they grow fairly rapidly, their eyes are not open until they are about four weeks of age. Then it takes another week or so before they leave the den and play about near the entrance.

At first they don't travel very far. If any of you have ever heard a woodchuck whistle, and they do this when danger is at hand, you know how sharp and piercing it is. When the youngsters hear it, they make a mighty effort to get out of sight and sometimes there is

a great amount of scrambling to see which one gets down the hole first. The average litter is about four, although this figure ranges as it does with all wild things.

I have always enjoyed them, even though they do raise considerable havoc with our garden. I don't know why, but I guess it is because I had a woodchuck as a pet once.

I was a student at Vermont Academy in the 1930s. A nearby farmer had dug out a den to remove the pests from his field and had saved this youngster, who hadn't yet had its eyes open, for the biology class. Of course, I volunteered to take care of it. Since when it first opened its eyes, it saw me instead of its mother, one of those strange things in Nature happened, called "imprinting." In other words, when it first opens its eyes whoever takes care of it, or it can cuddle up to, becomes its mother. Thus I became the mother of Chuckie.

When school was out that spring I took it home for the summer. Grandfather took to the little fellow at first sight. He delighted in feeding him—first, milk from a teaspoon as I had done at school, then bits of lettuce and, of all things, pieces of banana. If there ever was a spoiled woodchuck, it was Chuckie.

It was originally intended that he reside in the old henhouse which was no longer used, but he was such a lovable fellow that he came to spend his time in the house. We provided a box of sand in the back shed, as Chuckie was naturally housebroken.

He would follow Grandfather or me anywhere. We would walk

around the place or mow the lawn, or whatever, and he would be right behind. There was such a close relationship between man and animal that both Grandfather and I thought it certainly would have lasting qualities.

However, when fall came Chuckie began to dig a burrow. If we knew then what we know now, we would have let him. But we didn't, and we called him from his task with such regularity that he apparently became frustrated, for one day he disappeared. He came back the next day, after being out all night for the first time in his life. We didn't realize it, but that was the last time we were ever to see him. He had apparently found a home for himself. It was now late fall, the period of hibernation was near and he had eaten well during the summer so that he was ready for his long winter's sleep.

When spring came, we watched and hoped he might return. But he never did.

Woodchucks do make interesting pets and I think fondly of the days I spent with Chuckie. I do wonder how long this latest addition to the farm will stay in his den under the woodpile. I suppose not long, for as the lawn ceases to grow with springtime vigor he will have to forage greater distances for his food supply. Mildred, of course, is positive he will find the garden. I attempt half-heartedly to defend his present location but Mildred is probably right.

Night Sounds

THERE IS SOMETHING ABOUT THE NIGHT that emphasizes sound. Distant sounds come closer—near sounds grow louder.

When walking through a closed-in wood, a night sound makes one flutter. The unknown, the unseen, the mysterious, sets us to tingling. We are apt to be apprehensive of what we do not know. It is this uncertainty that gives us pause. An owl hooting at the right time, or perhaps I should say at the wrong time, can startle even the hardiest of souls.

Even so, I like to walk the woods at night. I follow a path through trees almost as easily as I can during the day. I look up toward the sky and I see the ground better than when I look directly at it. I can't explain why. There must be a good explanation, but I don't worry about what it is. All I know is, it works for me.

I walk softly and yet when my foot breaks a stick it seems as though the whole woods should wake. Sometimes my walking disturbs a slumbering bird and it will wake long enough to sing a chorus for me. Then it will go quiet and I presume tuck its head beneath its wing and fall asleep. When I get near the brook, I hear its music. How beautiful its singing! There is something lyrical about falling water.

And then there is rain.

In the daytime I see rain fall and, unless it is really pelting, I rarely hear it. But at night rain is loud. It is as though each drop were a tuning fork that had been hard struck.

When I lie in bed and listen through an open window, I seem to hear every drop hit a leaf. Then again, the rain comes all at once and the noise is all together. I picture in my mind swinging leaves as they're touched by the rain, dancing to a lively tune. The music is never monotonous for it is made of varied notes. The tempo changes, the sound changes. Now loud and rapid does the rain fall. Now slowly does the rain flow. And while the leaves tremble, the bark runs black.

And then I hear it in the distance—thunder. The rolling timpani comes closer. Then, as suddenly as a clashing cymbal, lightning scribbles across the sky. It lights the hillside bright, then brighter. In the light I see the trees begin to bend and weave—tossing branches holding leaves. Green glistens out of darkness. With such brilliance does the lightning flash that I see the reddened green of trees after black dark has come again.

A summer storm oft goes as quickly as it comes. And when all is quiet save but the lessening rain, a soothing silence covers the valley. Sleep comes easily.

Just before light begins to break, I often wake to the repetitious calling of a whippoorwill bidding farewell to night. His name spills easily from his mouth and is caught and exaggerated by the dark. How piercing his shriek. How still the woods when he is through!

Then one by one the morning birds awake. A robin carols. At first he hesitates for fear his speaking too soon will keep the night. He becomes bolder as dawn streaks the east. Now he knows the darkness will soon be gone. With new-found bravado he fairly hollers for all to hear. "Cheer-up—Cheer-ee. Cheer-up—Cheer-ee." Next the ovenbird, perhaps the noisiest of the wood warblers, screeches, "Teacher. Teacher." A startled blue jay casts a cry and then a scarlet tanager hoarsely greets the morn.

And so it goes—one bird and then another, and then a chorus and the morning is full of song. The night is fair forgotten.

Cutting the Winter's Wood

CUTTING THE WINTER'S WOOD is a chore I look forward to. I didn't use to when a lad, for then it was hard work trying to keep up with Grandfather on the end of a crosscut saw. I'd like a nickel for every red oak and maple I labored over.

There is a technique in working a crosscut. You just pull. You don't push. A morning on the end of a crosscut saw drags considerably when there is a baseball game to play on a summer's afternoon. So it was mighty hard to simply let the saw be dragged back without giving it a good shove. I was full of ginger in those days and although I recognized the need for a winter's supply of wood there was more of the grasshopper about me than the ant.

Grandfather would hitch up Dolly between the "sharves" of a flat-bed wagon, put the crosscut, sledge, wedge and Grandmother's bounteous lunch in back of the seat. And, along with these, a box of fence-fixing tools. Grandfather wanted to be prepared, for he knew that in mid to late August, when the pasture began to dry up, the cattle would often find the grass greener on the other side of the fence. Oh yes, we carried a small bag of salt to keep the cattle from becoming too friendly while the wood cutting was going on. It is startling, to say the least, when you are working the crosscut for all your worth and, without any warning, a cow blows in your ear.

We'd start out after breakfast for Oak Hill pasture. Dolly was a horse who went right along. I recall the grain bag cover over the wooden seat could have been thicker but I got used to it before summer vacation was over and, in retrospect, it wasn't too bad.

I liked the sound the wagon wheels made. I enjoyed traveling beneath the shady trees beside the river. I watched for birds along its bank and hoped to see a trout jump.

On bright August mornings, the cicadas would sing and Grandfather would say, "It's going to be a scorcher." He was always right, but the air was good and although memory dims the sting of mosquito and deer fly bites, I recall those trips fondly. Grandfather taught me to drive a horse at Oak Hill and it stood me in good stead years later.

When we arrived, Grandfather would jump off the wagon, unlock and open the gate. I'd take the reins, sit as tall as I knew how, and say with authority "Git up." Then I would attempt to create a chucking sound from the side of my mouth in imitation of Gramp's notification to the horse that she was to move forward. I realize now that the horse knew what she was about and my exhortations were really quite unnecessary, but it made me feel good to think I was doing the driving.

All this came back one Sunday in August when Mildred and I took the chain saw and our lunch to Oak Hill to cut fireplace wood.

I was working up the tops from the hardwood. The cutting was selective, for I only believe in taking the mature trees and leaving a good stand of growth for the future. Cutting over a piece does a great deal to promote wildlife. Because a forest is constantly changing, trees growing larger and more dense, the variety of birds also changes until "at climax" there are relatively few birds. As the forest is opened up, the birds move back.

While eating lunch, we heard two broad-winged hawks crying. We could see them floating against a deep blue sky. They were noisy so they must have fed recently. Broad-wings have a very high-pitched cry, almost like the wood pewee. A curious chipmunk scurried from behind one nearby stump to another, then bounced to the top of a boulder for a better look. "A people watcher," I mused.

Oak Hill has been in the Cole family for a long time. I have a packet of deeds, some of them handwritten, which prove the boundary lines. Originally, much of it was open land. Stone walls mark the bounds of the various parcels. They are interesting to see and wonder about. How the old-timers managed to build the walls so well intrigues me. I like Oak Hill. I enjoy going there.

Haying

Poets occasionally whisper about the smell of new mown hay as they brush soft words against a page. There is something soothing and perhaps a bit nostalgic about this delicate odor, something to nudge our past. Unknowingly, we are reminded of some misty day, years ago.

WHENEVER MY NOSTRILS gather in light-scented air from across a meadow where hay is making, I am quietly transported through time to a day in summer when life was indeed pleasant.

But as my thoughts point more toward the reality of that past time I recall the pace was not as leisurely as the memory. For, from the time when the cutter bar slashed the growing grass until the last forkful was mowed away in the bay, there was little time to pause and wonder at the beauty of haying. It was, in fact, a nervous time for me. Always with one eye to the heavens which I hoped would graciously withhold any hint of rain, I went forth with tractor-mounted mower to the meadow.

I liked to get started as early after milking as possible, for the grass cut better when fresh with dew. As long as a storm in its frivolity had not lodged the grass too much, the mowing was easy. There were places, though, where the spreading of too much hen litter had caused the grass to grow rank. It had lodged from its own weight. Here it was the cutter bar would break away and I'd have to back into it and clear the clog. It often took much longer to mow a swath than there seemed any need of and, not surprising, my remarks became a bit testy.

When the grass had been laid low the songbirds would gather to forage. I loved to watch the redwings and the meadow larks rise from the mowing when interrupted by the tractor's approach. The meadow larks would hang by their wings a little way off, then fall back to the field after the machine had passed. Redwings would go farther away but would return, several birds as one, with danger past.

My hay land was not always pure in its stand. There were discussion groups of daisies standing here and there. As the breeze came up, they would nod in agreement with each other. I never heard a cross word from them, or from the buttercups either, but the alders beside the meadow would scrape their leaves in protest against a darkening sky. I thanked them for their sympathy, for a rainstorm was no part of a good day's haying.

After cutting, it was time to do the conditioning, which was always a pleasure. All I had to do was sit on the tractor and drive over the hay swaths while the hay conditioner (sometimes called a crusher) lifted up the hay, passed it through two heavy rollers and windrowed it behind. The stems of the plants were crimped so they would dry in approximately the same time as the leaves. Haymaking was much speeded up with the advent of this machine. Years before, we used the tedder which kicked the hay up off the ground so the breezes of summer could assist in the drying. I prefer the more modern machine, for it gave time for musing.

My land lay beside the river and when my tractor took me near its bank I'd look for swimming beaver or muskrats. I never saw a beaver, although there were signs of them, but all day the muskrats would push mouthfuls of swale grass before them—and behind would be twin trails of riffling water.

In the field, always there were scurrying meadow mice and occasionally, sad to relate, evidences of one of them not making a safe place as they ran before the cutter bar. Later the crows would patrol and scavenge the area.

In the meadow the grass dies that the cows may live; mice die so crows may live; insects die that birds may live. This would have been so whether my mowing machine and I had been there or not. Life springs from death and circles round about. Sadness is fleeting on the meadow, for life is abundant there. New grass grows almost before the old is carted off. All will be well once more.

What beautiful patterns of light and shadow the clouds made passing before the sun! Sometimes the shadows would allow me to catch them as I went round and round. At other times they kept just ahead until they passed to the river bank and beyond. I'd be bathed in the warm sun until by its height I knew it was noon. It was time to sit in the cool of the river trees and unwrap my sandwich which, along with my thermos, had rested the morning in the shade. Somehow food need not be complicated to taste good after a morning in the meadow. Cold lemonade and buttered bread is food for a king in such a circumstance.

By afternoon, the meadow was full of the smell of drying hay—to me, one of the most delicate scents of the outdoors. It overrides the pungency of yarrow, the fleeting fragrance of wild roses, the river smells. It grows stronger toward evening and, as the fogs rise, is carried to the hills and seems everywhere to be.

I like the smell of haying.

Late August

ALL DAY WARM AIR CONSPIRED with oppressive humidity, and the two filled the valley. Toward evening these companions had crowded into the cool places beneath pines that sheltered the slow-running brook. The damp air made mists rise and caused the sky to fill with haze. The hills at the north and west assumed the appearance of a pastel painting. Dark green leaves of oak and maple merged with lighter shades of other hardwoods and endowed the hills with a rolling softness.

Tall pines at the skyline appeared as feather plumes that had been carefully pushed into the hilltop by an old Indian chieftain creating a headdress to befit his greatness. The big, round, orange sun clung to the feathery pines, attempting to hold its place and the daylight. But its time had come. However, as it retreated, it drew a number of arrows from its quiver and sprayed flaming color shafts through the treetops, piercing the haze. Beyond the haze, over the hills, immense clouds were mere sketch-lines as the sun reflected their edges. Through a hazy patch the blue sky, high above, made a bright lake.

I was admiring the soft, gentle beauty of the sky when, suddenly, like a shake of pepper, the blue lake was dotted with fast-flying birds. It was a flock of nighthawks in migration, flying in concert. There were more than a hundred, circling and floating, swerving and darting, feeding on insects as they went.

It was the last day of August and for several evenings nighthawks had been on the move. They had drifted over the farm in groups of three or five. No doubt they came from the city where during the summer they had increased the night noises with their nasal cries. Flying through our valley the nighthawks seemed almost bewildered. They were quiet and hardly more than loafing through the sky. They gave no indication of having a destination but when they went it was southward.

It was then I noticed that the shaded line drawings of the clouds had turned to pink-white and the clouds had taken on more substance. First they appeared as solemn, snow-capped mountains. Then they changed into fluffy animal forms and stalked one another.

After the sun ball had dropped behind the hills, blue and purple hues were turned loose—a compromise between daylight and darkness.

The Butterfly

An orange butterfly alighted near my eye,
As it folded up its wings
I thought I heard it sigh,
"I'd like to stay and visit
But the day is nearly spent."
Quietly it arose
And then, decided, went.

I WATCHED A BUTTERFLY ALIGHT upon a nodding milkweed pod and carefully fold his wings. And when he had caught his breath I asked, "Where have you been, my friend?" And before he had time to answer I inquired, "Where will you go from here?"

He shuddered just a bit and then, waving one antenna in quizzical gesture, lifted into the air, and whirling roundabout with uncertainty finally fluttered off without an answer to my query. Perhaps one question at a time should have been enough, but I wanted to know where he'd been and where he'd go. But it was none of my affair. After all, a butterfly's business is his more than mine.

I guess I hoped he'd say, "I come from your childhood. I am the one you chased and never caught. I've never been caught. I don't intend to become a prisoner of even myself. I just do what I do, without reason or cause, or, for that matter, effect. It is only humans who have to have an explanation for everything."

"Why" is one of the first words we learn and "why" is why we do

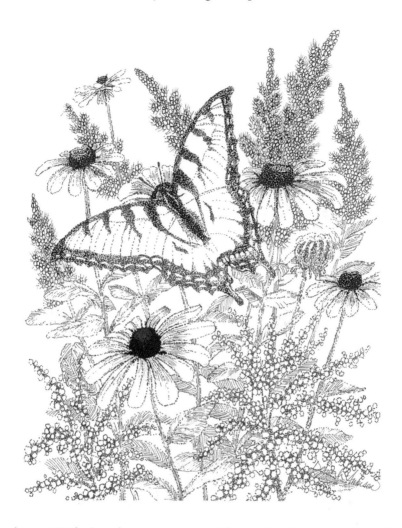

things. "Why" perhaps answers itself. But all this is butterfly talk and while my mind was conversing with the passing Danaid my mind was wandering back to where I'd been. My childhood days came to view and stared back at me.

I saw myself chasing a butterfly in the great meadow at Grandfather's farm. While he generally didn't appreciate anyone bumbling through his uncut hay, he never chastised me for my wanderings. He liked me to look at wild things and get to know the ways of the outdoors. So it has been for most of my life. The outdoors has been good to me and good for me. It has been there that I have enjoyed life most.

I have especially enjoyed those creatures who were not earth-bound. And I learned that I, too, was not earth-bound. It only appeared so. I could soar as high as the farthest cloud—and beyond where the clouds disappeared. For wings, my imagination.

When I climbed the maple tree beside the railroad track I was nearer heaven. Heaven sent, you might say. I could talk to clouds and watch the nesting robins who were tied to earth part of their time. They fed at earth. They taught their young there. They rested in trees and on man-made things. Yes, they, too, were earthbound part of the time. If so, why couldn't I be heaven-bound part of the time? And so I was.

When the trains to Boston went by, I'd wave to the engineer. In summer, no one could see me there, but in spring and fall I was easy to find. In winter I didn't go there. Yes, I liked to wave to the passing magnificence that was the train. How strong the engines were that hauled the cars with such ease! Except when the freight was too heavy for slippery rails and then the locomotive's chugging would increase until one chug ran into another and the engine's drivers would have to get another grip.

When the trains passed beyond my sight and hearing, a part of me went with them. Oh, there were times I stayed to keep the robins company, but there were other times when I went along with the engineer to protect him from robbers. I don't know how many train robbers I caught after a mighty struggle when my wits outwitted their wits. It was fun to be a hero. There was little I could not do when sitting in my tree.

There were other places for meditation. One was the hill in back of the house where spring started from winter and developed into summer. I loved the hill, ever changing, both to see and to be with. On a March day I would hide from the sharp north wind behind a grey boulder. I'd listen for the first warblings of the bluebirds. They seemed to arrive before the robins. Their happy springtime notes, different from their plaintive tones in fall, would enthrall me. Spring brought the smell of mayflowers, a brighter hue to the sky, thoughts of baseball, and the time when school would be out. It was then I could come to the hill every day, even on rainy days, to watch the rain drop from leaf to leaf until it finally hit the ground. From the hill on a summer evening the whitethroats would tell about "Old Sam Peabody." I wondered about him. Was there ever such a man? I was sure there was.

In childhood everything is possible. If not today, then some day. I guess that's when I first became acquainted with "some day." I've been looking forward to gaining upon it but never really getting there, for there is much more in anticipation than in looking back.

But today I have looked back. Unless I could pick and choose, I wouldn't want to go back. I want to search for "some day," but I hope I'll never find it.

A Magic Memory Ride

ONCE UPON A TIME beneath a cloudless sky, I lay feet downward on a hillside and let my eyes unfocus. Somewhere there were sounds that told of others less preoccupied than I. They were doing something. I was doing nothing.

The soft spring smells of evening passed me by, but left their scent on me as though I were a bended branch too full of leaves. 'Twas then I was stirred to thinking. Why not get up, run downhill, spread my arms and soar backwards into time—take a magic memory ride?

Why not, indeed?

So I rose and ran and flung my arms outward. My mind was strong enough to overcome gravity and I lifted ever so slightly. Then by increasing thought I gained the air and was almost free of earth when, passing over a farmhouse in the valley my right toe caught a brick, weather-loosened at the chimney top, and sent it clattering down inside. Somehow I knew it turned in its plunge to miss a nest of swifts. Then it struck the bottom with a thud. It roused the farmer from his doze.

"What's that?" he said, then dropped his head toward his lap once more. Come fall, he'd remember. He'd find the brick inside the cleanout door when scooping soot.

Instead of evening darkening into night, the day ran back upon itself. The sun walked backwards through the sky.

Looking down, I saw familiar ground. Land that hadn't been

cleared of trees for half a lifetime was open pasture. Cattle grazed nearby. The watering trough, cast in cement two generations ago, showed plain. Bright new fences, drawn tight so's to gain respect of cattle, ran the boundaries.

And then I saw them, walking slowly. Old settlers now, even in this young land, carrying fence tools in their hands, heading toward the shed to drop them there. Then to the house to fill a dipper with water from the spring. And let the water run cool down parched throats.

The kitchen sink was black iron cleaned well to keep it from rusting. The kitchen stove was black iron and polished to keep it from rusting. Beside the stove was the woodbox with top opened back. Whether it was half empty or half full, I don't remember. It would depend on whether wood was wanted to be carried or not. The kitchen table, without cloth, held salt, pepper, vinegar cruse and sugar bowl. The floorboards, uncovered, showed clean, bright wood in the afternoon sun. They ran lengthwise of the room to where the worn-down threshold led outside. Curtains at the open window blew in softly. I could smell an apple pie baking. Somehow I knew it had been made from dried apples soaked and readied the night before. This was the old kitchen of my boyhood.

Before I left I wanted to look at the parlor once more, shut up except for special times. A mysterious place where everything was just the same as when first placed there. The couch had an afghan thrown over it. Hard, plump pillows, dressed in needlepoint of intricate design, were placed at each end. The parlor never smelled like the kitchen or any other part of the house for that matter. It was kept shut up and had an air of its own. The last time I'd been there I had heard sobbing. Now the echo from the walls bespoke it.

So I turned and shut the door and, passing, glanced into the bedroom and saw the bed. I looked at the great cherry headboard and the lesser cherry footboard. I remembered the hard feel of the tight-roped canvas beneath the feather bed. A blue comforter was thrown across it, smoothed to cover to the pillows. Blue wallpaper bordered in white ran the room. The blue room, they'd called it.

Then, through the kitchen with a final glance, I went outside and once more astride my dream I rose and followed the road to town.

I passed over neighbors' farms and remembered when we'd go that way with horse and wagon. We'd wave and smile the smile of friendship, knowing that when we needed help they'd be ready to lend a hand. Neighboring was important then.

Folks learned to depend upon one another without weakening themselves. There is a difference in using help and leaning with a heavy weight to bring others down to where the load has bent.

Then I saw the steeple, white, pointed skyward. Pointing above the hills. Pointing with promise. Faith would seal the bargain. Faith would build the world.

I don't exactly remember how I got back to the hillside from whence I started, but I was there. I'd been gently lifted and gently returned. The sun was nearly set and in the valley mists were rising.

This time, when I stood I walked. There was no need to fly. The ground felt good to my feet. I'd had enough of sleep.

Chinook and I

Over the years we have always had a dog, sometimes two—never three. They were all good ones. That is, we got to love them as much as dogs can be loved. There were times when we had to convince them they were not people and times when we had to remember they were dogs. Such is the way it is with a farm family. But there were some traits that endeared each of them to us and, as recollection would have it, Chinook was very special. When the vet introduced him to Mildred (I was away on a trip on Farm Bureau business) he said, "He's sort of like a collie." And so he was. But he was like "a sled dog," too, at least that's the way I saw him. And so I named him after Admiral Byrd's famous lead dog. I'd been to Wonalancet once to see his dogs. That was a long time ago.

CHINOOK AND I WENT FOR A WALK TODAY. We went down the pasture lane, through the open gate, and there we stopped. We stood beneath a maple and looked across small fields we called pasture. They had been so used for a quarter century, until this summer, and thus earned the name.

Chinook sat at my feet and joined in the looking. Things were different now. There were no cows feeding, no bright green, no fall rain-fresh grass growing within stone-wall fences. Instead, wind-bent, low-lying, untrampled, uncut, tangled brown grass met our gaze.

I was shocked.

Chinook looked at me. I puzzled him, but not the dying grass, for he'd seen it grow brown with summer's passing. Most every day since spring he'd hunted woodchucks there.

For many years Chinook had traveled the pasture lane behind the cows. Down in the cool damp of the morning after milking, back at night. We'd meet the cows at the bars and follow them up to the barn. All spring and summer and fall—'way beyond frost time—we'd "take" or "get" the cows. But not again, our farming days were done.

The pasture looked it. That's why I was shocked. That's why I puzzled Chinook. He'd worn what path there was and had become used to the pasture as it now was. I'd spent my summer without going down the lane and so I remembered what had been. I wasn't ready for what was there.

The crickets and crows called fall. Somehow I wasn't ready for the death of summer.

I looked to the still green hills and saw the red and orange sparks that soon would kindle the woodland into flame. A goldfinch waved its way across the pasture and alighted on a thistle.

I remembered. I would not forget.

But I would not do any more the things in spring and every day that would bring back the pasture green. Soon I'd watch fall in flame. I'd watch bright leaves turn dull, depart the trees and flutter to the ground. I'd be a watcher, not a doer.

Dead grass and dead leaves will disappear as winter comes. There'll be another spring when tree toads will "shout from the mists." I'll wait 'til then.

The goldfinch was to blame for the memories that mingled and stirred in a moment's reflection.

But the beauty of today is now.

Robert Frost once said, "We love the things we love for what they are."

"He's right," I mused.

An Intruder

AT THE LOWER EDGE of our young pine forest we have a few shagbark hickories. The shagbark is a magnificent tree that lends a wild, rugged, almost irregular beauty to our forest. They are elegant trees, especially during the late days of November when their inky-black, leafless boughs appear as an etching against the sky.

Years ago, Grandfather used to cut hickory whenever he needed a new supply of axe helves or a wagon tongue. The wood is close-grained and tough, nearly as strong as iron. It also makes good firewood as it burns brightly, lasts a long time and gives off good heat.

One morning, while walking toward the farmhouse from the upper henhouse, I was startled by the loud, excited calling of crows. My first thought was that this alarm was being sounded to warn that a red fox had traveled from his den in the ledges, down through the pine forest, in search of his next meal, and had been sighted by our three crows that watchfully patrol the farm.

These three crows have been with us for several years. They are our constant companions as we go about our field work during spring, summer and fall. They follow the plough in the spring and check the land for white grubs. They walk and hop through meadows and pastures during the summer, feeding on grasshoppers. They nest in the tall pines back of the barn and teach their young how to forage for themselves. In late fall, after the young have departed, the three neighbor together and call attention from time to time to matters that upset them.

I looked toward the hickories where the racket was apparently originating. I saw nothing, yet the din was increasing. Suddenly one of the crows flew from behind the tallest hickory and was immediately followed by the other two.

But wait! The first was being chased by the two. This was highly unusual for these three were fast friends. As they circled and twisted and fought their way closer it became evident that the first crow was much larger than the other two. Impossible! Even young crows are not that much smaller than their parents and, besides, their young had long since grown and flown to other territories.

The larger one swung higher and flapped across the highway toward the river with the others in hot pursuit. The two crows giving chase were now joined by a third. The mystery heightened!

The pursued began to soar. At this I wondered if I had been mistaken in believing he was black. Perhaps I had been fooled by the grey sky. But when the big fellow suddenly dodged and flew back, coming in lower, directly overhead, he was indeed solid black. I knew then what he was.

He gave up the chase, flying down river until he disappeared from our valley.

The wind sprang up in the pines and I was sure I heard "the silken sad uncertain rustling" of the boughs. There had been a raven in our valley and at the rate he had withdrawn one could almost hear him sigh—"Nevermore."

October Snow

WOOD SMOKE SPILLED AND CURLED from the big, square chimney of the farm house and drifted among the tiny snowflakes that were hardly more than disappearing visions. The smell of the smoke mingled with the snow's dampness and dulled the edge of the sharp wind.

Late October snows are often but a whim of Nature, yet when they are carried into the valley by a capricious wind they hint a promise of days to come. In the big farm kitchen the damper gets turned in the fireplace, bits of crumpled paper and kindling are laid, and the first flames become jubilant as they dance away cobwebby shadows.

In the meadows the flocking robins work at their feeding with a sudden urgency. Gone is their leisurely hopping, listening and probing. Now there is a ravenous craving to be answered. They are seized with a need to stuff themselves before the thickening snows make feeding a difficult chore.

The birds seem to sense the possibility of having their supply of food cut off by a period of wild weather. Folks who have bird feeding stations near their homes can become quite adept at predicting the weather simply by watching bird activity.

Just before a storm the chickadees and nuthatches will make more frequent visits, eating great quantities of seeds, especially sunflower seeds. The blue jays will fairly bloat their throats with seeds and fly rapidly to their shelter in the deep woods. Downy and hairy woodpeckers normally will not tolerate one another, or even one of their own kind, too close at the suet cage, but just before a storm they are often observed eating side by side.

Impending trouble allows a place for cooperation against a common foe in nature as it does with man.

The Arrival of Winter

THE SKY WAS GREY AND DENSE. Its somber, shapeless shroud veiled the early afternoon light. The first snow was falling and its quiet gentleness spread silence through the valley.

The tiny flakes were damp and clinging. They caught on pine limbs and piled into conforming ridges. The snow clustered at the places where the pine needles started from the slender branches. It grew toward the needle ends as they sprayed outward and clung tightly, changing green rays into silver beams.

The snow grew heavy and bent the branches, softening the shape of the pine. The minute flakes dropped to cover dead brown goldenrod blossoms. They overflowed the cup of the wild carrot's closed head and slipped from the purple smoothness of the raspberry canes that entwined the weed patch.

The snow fell to the ground briars, flaking their reddish-brown leaves with white and hiding their sharp spines. The snow covered the ground, except for the rocks. There, the snow melted as it hit and caused black pools amid the profusion of white.

The shattered and twisted milkweed pods, emptied of their own puffy, white cotton fluff, contentedly gathered snow to replace their loss. A recently fallen white pine cone rested lightly on the branch of a pasture juniper. The cone was dark brown and slightly curved. Its scales were full open to welcome the snow. Winter had set in.

A Moonlight Stroll

I WENT OUT TO HEAR AN OWL HOOT. It was within two hours of midnight and I was sure an owl would be abroad, for the night was clear, lighted with a brilliant moon. All shadows stood still.

I'd been watching television and had become weary of that amusement when the idea struck. About an hour earlier, I'd fixed the wood fire out in the back room. When I'd looked out the window, the moonlight was so bright it had dimmed the stars. The trees were motionless and the shadows lay quiet upon the snow blanket.

I'm not sure but if there had been tossing shadows I'd have thought twice about going out. Such movements at night, especially in the dead of night, can sometimes start the hairs on the back of my neck. This phenomenon is usually accompanied by an uneasy tingling along my spine. It's not that I'm afraid exactly, but I have always been apprehensive about unseen things that toss shadows at my head. And creaking things, when there is no cause for them to creak.

But it was this memory of a night full of peace that impelled me to jump up from the Boston rocker and announce, "I'm going out to hear an owl hoot!"

Mildred was doing needlepoint beside the hearth and when I spoke, she didn't miss a stitch. She was not surprised. I didn't really expect her to be, for we've lived together long enough so that she has become quite used to my impetuosity.

"You going to take the dog?" she asked.

"Nope. 'Fraid he'd make too much noise sniffin' after rabbits or trying to outwit that red fox that hangs around the brook," I said, while putting on muffler, greatcoat, cap and mittens.

I left the house and further conversation at the same time.

I looked at the moon and saw it hadn't quite reached the top of the sky. My shadow paced along beside, or I supposed it did. I hadn't paid much mind to it until I passed a wall. Then it jumped upright and we walked with the same pair of boots. It was a good thing we did, for the noise of one pair was enough. Any owl would certainly have known by this time that someone was abroad. If the footfalls hadn't aroused him, he would have heard the soft calling of the cattle as we passed by the barn. They wanted me to come in and sweep up the hay they'd pushed too far in the manger to reach. We often did that, but tonight I just wanted to get into the woods and smell cold air and pine. I'd had enough of indoors.

But when I reached the woods, I couldn't smell the pine. Too cold, I remember thinking. I tried to walk with muffled step but crusted snow would have no part of that. A pair of boots and frozen snow can make an unbelievable amount of conversation.

The moon was playing peek-a-boo in the tops of pines. Whenever I looked for it, it always seemed part hidden. But then I fooled it by standing still. And while I waited, half listening for an owl, the moon slipped into the open. How bright it was and how beautiful it caused the trees to be! The last snowfall had clung to them. Branches of hardwoods, hemlock and pine had all caught their share and, with Jack Frost's help, had held it.

When sunlight strikes snow it sends a shower of sparks at you, like a chain being dragged along a hard-topped road. Moonlight doesn't seem to do that. Its brightness isn't bright enough to split the colors locked in snow into the million fragments that sunlight seems to do. Beauty, I mused, shows itself in many ways—occasionally in striking ways, but mostly unobtrusively. And ofttimes when you see it you wonder why you've never seen it there before.

The path took me beside the brook. It spoke softly as it found its way beneath the ice. I could barely hear it. As I climbed the path, the water tumbled down from high above. The brook wasn't speaking now. It had burst into song. I wished I could place a clef and line a page, and make the half notes, quarter, eighth and full notes, slurs and other marks that would allow man to interpret such melody as came to me. But my talent does not run that way. I can only borrow a few words, which have been used by writer and poet alike, to try to say what the brook said. Truth is, I must confess I don't know what the brook said. But what it said, it sang each note in harmony with its world. And I was a part of its world.

Various thoughts cross a body's mind when alone. I guess that's the reason one needs time to oneself. As I walked the familiar path that wound upwards between two hills, it occurred to me that it really wasn't an owl I'd come to hear. It was silence that I'd sought—that natural quietness that one hardly ever hears. And when one does, it has a sudden shout.

And so it was this night. Silence spoke and what I heard were my innermost thoughts coming back to me.

What was this time? It was now. And I was here and surrounded by such beauty as no one before had ever seen. I was sure of that.

Tall birches reached for the moonlight that the pines wanted to keep for themselves. The birches were just as bright at night as they were in day, except their form was more leaning, bent by snow as if it were more burden to them than to the other trees. Pines let the weight of snow bend them down. Rarely do the loads bear more on pines than they can take, except when ice storms hit. Even then, it is more the leafless trees that bend to breaking and leave ragged white wood exposed and left to bleed when spring comes. Pines carry their burdens well. I admire them for it.

Strange, ofttimes those that seem least likely to stand a strain can do so best. They have an inner strength, I think, that bears them up when most would fail. It is that inner strength that man must find.

I like to walk the hills at night. I like to have the shadows stand still and not give me a fright. But most of all I like to hear the silence, the quiet—the speaking as from the heart.

The January Thaw

Frost will not split stone tonight.
Pine trees will not crack.
Soothing, soft wind will sing in flight
While winter, stifled, is thrown back.

THE JANUARY THAW is a most pleasant time—when tidings of the coming season of spring are heralded by chickadees chatting to one another and, for that matter, for all to hear.

I've noticed, or thought I had, a difference in chickadee musings as spring is entering. A more thankful, sibilant series of notes seems to come from these lovable, black and white birds as the longer days turn warm. (The "thankful" may be wishful thinking on my part.)

When you walk along a country road and feel the last biting blush of winter and pass from cold air against your cheek to a warmer, gentler touch, you sometimes can sift a smell of spring from a light stirring of air. How elusive it is! I've often stopped to catch its flavor and found it had hurried by and was about to turn the corner passed. I've noticed this in January thaw and looked for this phenomenon with delight. Don't hasten to think I am disappointed at not always finding the scent of spring in January, for I'm really not. But the hope ever joins me, just the same.

Why do I say the January thaw is announced by chickadees? Nothing you can put a practical finger upon, I suppose, but rather there seems a noticeable tone change in their familiar voice. In cold winter clarity, our chickadees busy themselves about the corners of the house where lilacs toss and scratch the clapboards. The birds are constantly conversing in most pleasant tones. Of their voices, Bent says, "The prettiest note of all, and the most delicate, is a prolonged jingling—as if tiny, silver sleigh bells were shaking."

When they talk of January thaw, they sound softer, more respectful of what may be. This time is before the groundhog is supposed to stretch and creep from dark den to light, to see how much light and pronounce it good enough for six more weeks of sleep. This time is before buds should swell, turn red and prepare to burst. Though if the January thaw lasts long enough, perhaps they might be fooled into doing just that. I hope not, for I don't like things to happen sooner than is natural. Flowers are not forever, nor should buds break before winter does.

Sunrise streaks red across the sky and bathes the hills in wine. Heavy, sculpturesque clouds, still black with night-drape background, silhouette the birch—then let the morning in. The valley, washed in opening light, shows wetness over everything—melting air and melting snow—softening footfalls for whoever goes a-wandering.

The new day cracks whatever ice cool night hands have molded. It lifts the ice in rivers and parts the way for tumbling, roiling, rushing water now set free. It shouts against boulders. It rumbles beneath bridges. It proclaims a change in mood. And, as the sun ball rises to take its place in day, the chickadees rejoice and chatter as though spring really were on its way.

I wonder if these cheerful birds get "cabin bound" as men are wont to do, wishing they were somewhere else, with something else to do? Scientists would no doubt scoff at my taking liberties with chickadees. "Their thoughts are mostly instinctive or early learned," they'd say. But maybe once, or maybe twice, could chickadees not be permitted to weave a thought, as I'd want to do if I were they—out singing, proclaiming a day of January thaw?

I wonder.

With the chickadees, I feel the sun's warmth and stand idly by and watch it take water from the snow as mere pirates' plunder.

For some, January thaw is a mid-season miracle, a pleasant oasis in winter. For others who prefer chill cold and blowing snows, it is no time at all. But whatever, or whoever, that's the way of Nature. And so we accept it and, if we can, rejoice and say, "This day was one borrowed from Spring."

Winter Wind

There is nothing that makes me want to stay in the house more than when winter is full blown and a storm is swinging the leafless branches.

THE WINTER WIND BELLOWED its belligerence and carried its quarrelsome whine from the topmost ledge of the northern hill into our valley. There was not a tree or bush nor stiff-stemmed shrub that did not bend before the merciless monarch. The wind was not to be stayed for this was its unconquerable day.

The snow that traveled in company with the wind conspired with the snow that had come before. Together they danced an irregular swirling reel to the tune of a moaning lament. The snow swept swiftly across fields. Some slammed against stone walls and filled the crevices, becoming firm, solid chinking.

The weed stems were dipped low and tossed hard against the deepening snow as the wind bullied them and spilled their seeds. The wind came from everywhere and it went everywhere.

The hills beyond the meadows were to be seen only at the whim of the wind, whenever it chose to rest the snow dancers while it improvised a new air. The sky turned darker as the storm furrowed its brow. A grey-white world waited for the angry wind to pass.

Two large lilac bushes sprawl against our back shed wall. During the storm, their leafless limbs composed a somber strain as they scratched against the window panes. Beneath the lilacs a small flock of juncos and tree sparrows clasped weed stalks and attempted to feed on the seeds. In seeming mockery the wind tossed the stalks with the clinging birds and scattered the weed seeds with the snow. Now and again a bird would drop to the ground and scratch a pocket in the snow, searching for seeds.

Although it hardly seemed possible for a bird to fly in the face of such an adversary, a flock of a half-dozen chickadees appeared from out of the storm and clung to the lilacs' whipping branches. They took turns swinging with the red sunflower-seed feeder wired to a branch. They would grasp a seed in their beak and dodge to a nearby limb. Once their footing was secured they would tuck the seed under one foot while they pried open the shuck with their bill.

The birds apparently had no further appointments that day, for they could be seen during the daylight hours scrambling from branch to feeder and back again. Just before darkness became complete, one by one, they took wing against the fury of the storm in search of shelter for the night.

The storm raged on until during the early morning hours—the wind and the darkness departed together.

The Day the Chicks Came

AS FEBRUARY COMES INTO VIEW each year, I think of chickens.

The first chicks I ever bought arrived on the 20th of February. It was a clear, cold day. Snow had fallen during the night and by mid-morning the wind had not unfrocked the trees. Each fence post wore a jaunty cap and the pines on the hillside were fully gowned.

Down in the field nearest the house were seven brand-new brooder houses. Each house had a coal-burning brooder stove set on a galvanized sheet so the hot coals couldn't set the wood floor ablaze when the ashes were taken out. The stoves had metal hovers which directed the heat toward the floor.

A couple of days before the chicks arrived, I had started the stoves. Wood shavings were placed on the floor for bedding. Over this we placed newspapers. You see, when baby chicks first come they pick at anything they find handy, and we didn't want them to eat shavings. We placed cracked corn on the papers and in addition we had chick feeders radiating from the stove like the spokes of a wheel.

The day the chicks were due finally came. I had been glancing up the road anxiously since daybreak. A little before eight o'clock, although it seemed later than that to me, a small panel truck drove into the yard and a most happy greeting was exchanged between Mr. Ira S. Hubbard, founder of Hubbard Farms, Walpole, N.H., and myself. He opened the back door of the truck and handed out the first of fifteen boxes which held one hundred baby chicks each. (Hubbard always added a few extra to give a good count.)

When the sled was loaded I threw an old quilt over the boxes and drew the sled to the nearest brooder house. Mr. Hubbard and I used both hands as a scoop and gently lifted and placed the chicks, four or five at a time, beneath the hovers. How those tiny balls of yellow fluff did scamper about! They would stop and pick at the corn on the papers and drink from the fountains. And while we watched, some would stop in their tracks and camp down for a nap. At first, chicks sleep a lot, then they gradually stay active most of the time.

I look back with great pleasure to that visit with Ira Hubbard, and to the ones that followed over the years. He always enjoyed coming down on the farm and we certainly looked forward to having him. He was a gentle, quiet-spoken man possessed of great wisdom tempered with common sense. I liked him.

As the years went by, our operation grew. We built a special building to grow chicks, using gas for heat and automatic feeders. A more efficient time had come, but it is those earlier days of harder work that will be remembered kindly. The days when Ira Hubbard came with baby chicks were very special days.

The Ice Storm

There comes a time in winter and before spring when Nature is not quite sure what she wants. It is in this questioning, restless mood that I believe she sends forth an ice storm.

THE AIR WARMED DURING THE AFTERNOON and softened the snow cover. Light rain began to fall and small streams started across the snow fields, wriggling their way to the valley runs.

Toward evening, the streams slowed their pace, then stopped altogether while the rain formed a crust over the snow. The air cooled as night came on. The rain did not retreat from the branches but lingered to form ice. The branches became encased, held secure by the growing sheath.

The rain continued to fall and was blown by the wind against the trees where it filled bark crevices and overflowed in tiny cascades, making glassy trails down the trunks.

When morning came it found that night had carelessly tossed a blanket of grey over the valley. Nearly all of the sky was layered with heavy clouds. Just above the shoulder of the wooded hill, to the northwest, morning painted a shaft of blue and hinted a promise of a brighter day.

The sun pushed the clouds away and revealed a silver-tinseled valley of sparkling fields and glistening trees. The hillside that had grown without pattern or plan was turned into a splendid setting of simple beauty. Black limbs, glazed with ice, reflected the sunlight as they swayed with formal grace in the wind.

On branch tips, bulblets of ice were created. Dainty icicles marked the water paths rain had chosen in its attempted escape. Bright sun made colors dance along small branches—blue-white swirled to orange-red, then green and blue, to blue-white again.

The crusted snow broke wide around each footfall and did so with a quick, sharp shatter. The under-snow whispered a soft hush. Near the path dried goldenrod was preserved in glass.

For the moment, the ice storm held fast.

The Time to Plough Has Come

For as long as I can remember, I have had a love affair with the land. I like its look in all seasons. I like its smell, its touch. But there is no time Down on the Farm when I love the land more than in spring when the time to plough has come.

THE TIME TO PLOUGH has come. The land, now free of frost and moistened by spring rain, waits to be tilled.

Days before ploughing, I watched spring rain fall in straight, grey lines from the overcast. I saw it lightly brush the grass a brighter green. A whispered message seemed to pass from the hiding sun— an appeal to brighten earth so that the wanderer would be dazzled by the change.

Rain falls. Earth receives. And the two join to release the power of life.

After the weather cleared, I drove my tractor to the field and dropped the plough. The damp, dark earth was cleaved and turned and in the turning buried last year's stubble, weeds and stalks. It made fog grass and creeping briars disappear. The tangle was covered deep, there to molder and be consumed so life could survive. How orderly the plough does work. Its colter cuts the cluttered sod and lets the ploughshare roll the earth and lay it bare. Fresh soil, moist and shining, lies in the sun.

The tractor followed beside the fence until it reached the headland and then turned and once more crossed the field. Back and forth, using the day to lay one furrow upon the shoulder of another until the whole field is ploughed.

While ploughing I like to watch the grackles search furrow bottoms for grubs and worms. They walk along ahead and when I get too close, they open their beaks to cry, but their voices are drowned by the engine sound. It may be thanks they speak or it may be they repine and squawk annoyance at being disturbed. When the tractor gets too close they take wing, hover a few feet ahead and having no more than gotten settled are driven off again. As we near the headland, the birds fly behind and continue searching. I turn the tractor to reverse direction and once more disturb the birds.

Thus we pass the afternoon—the tractor, the grackles and I. We work together really, for I prepare the soil to serve my needs and they search for food to serve themselves.

How good the field looks—fresh ground turned for a fresh start. The brown soil contrasts against the bright green meadow that lies across the run. I like to take up the fresh ploughed soil and hold it and breathe its dampish smell. And when I do, I know that life began here and can ever be renewed here.

A man needs to do his ploughing and to know the story of the land. He needs to remember there is a season for a new beginning.

A Weighty Decision

THE OTHER DAY Mildred said, "Let's raise some pigs."

I pretended I didn't hear her. Not that I have anything against pigs, quite the contrary, I think very highly of these animals. It's just that their care and feeding is somewhat of a nuisance,

She repeated her suggestion, believing I really hadn't heard her the first time.

"Pigs?" I replied. "You don't mean it."

"Yes. I do mean it," was her retort, and the ball being back in my court so's to speak, I floundered around for a good reason not to embark on a pig raising project.

My answer needed some thought. I didn't want to discourage her from doing something she really wanted to do, but on the other hand, another project might prove more to my liking. So I countered with a question. After all one does not have to be a psychologist to answer a question with a question.

"Where are you going to keep the pigs?" I inquired.

Knowing full well that our barn had burned to the ground over a year ago and that our original pig pen was across a busy highway and in a state of disrepair.

"Down under the apple trees," was her reply.

Hmmm, now that was not really a bad suggestion and was hard to counter, but I was still game. "Golly," I said, "that's right next to the garden and I have never known pigs to be raised anywhere on this farm that they didn't get out of the pen." I hoped she would remember how mad she got when the last batch of pigs rooted up a good portion of her garden.

She paused, but was not to be outdone, "I still think it would be a good idea."

I didn't answer right away, hoping that during the period of silence she would remember some of the other experiences we'd had with pig raising.

She might recall the time I was sitting at my desk and out of the corner of my eye I saw three men in white shirts sitting on our front lawn. Suddenly it occurred to me that that was most unlikely. Upon direct gaze, I discovered that three, nearly grown porkers, who, I had believed, were happily sleeping within the confines of their pen had escaped and were sitting in a row on the lawn watching the traffic pass by, as a car would appear in the distance, all three heads would face in that direction. Upon its approach and passing, the three heads would follow its progress until it faded from view. It was a hot summer's afternoon and they were perfectly comfortable sitting in the shade of the maple, watching the world pass by.

Probably that was not what Mildred would remember, for I was home alone and had the pleasure of encouraging the critters back into their pen. My recollection of that incident leaves little happiness to remember.

I picked up a hoe as I went through the shed and took off after the pigs. They decided it would be nice to head for the village instead of back to their abode. I followed them down the road for nearly a quarter mile before I was able to get ahead of them and turn them about.

As we neared the farm, I slackened my speed briefly and thought, certainly, the three would have had enough of traveling and would make for their pen. Not so. They kept right on going up Route 10 toward Keene. The four of us picked up speed at that point and we did another quarter mile in record time. Local traffic recognized my plight and smiled and waved encouragement as they cautiously passed the three and me. Transient traffic laughed outright and sped right along.

Finally, I gained on the porkers and turned them once again back toward the farm. This time they left the highway and took off through the woods in the general direction of the barn. Well, I won't go into further details, but suffice it to say, some time later I managed to corral them in their pen. They had loosened a couple of boards in their outside yard to make their escape. Needless to relate, I secured that part of their fence with spikes and expletives.

"Wouldn't you like some nice thick pork chops and fresh smoked hams?" Mildred inquired.

She knows how much I can be tempted with this kind of talk. And it might have worked except, once again, my memory was too long.

It was years ago, not long after we had scraped the bristles from our first pig and were soaking the bacon, shoulders and hams in brine Mildred had made up, when we realized that the builders of our house had allowed for smoking such products by constructing a smoke house as part of the brickwork in our cellar. It was vented into the big central chimney.

So, we thought, why not utilize it? We gathered some hickory wood from the woodpile and when the hams and bacon were ready, we hung them in the smoke house and started a small fire within the brick enclosure. The hickory did just what it was supposed to do. It smoked beautifully.

We were mighty proud of ourselves until a couple of days later when we went into our clothes closet upstairs. Heavens to Betsy! All of our clothes were hickory smoked, too! We smelled like walking hams for some time after that.

I was about ready to remind Mildred of that experience when a neighbor came to call and our conversation was interrupted. I hope that's the end of our discussion about raising pigs again, but somehow I kind of doubt it.

Yarn Spinning

WHEN TWO OLD POULTRYMEN get together, yarns are apt to be spun. As with most yarns, the truth may be slightly exaggerated occasionally, but only for emphasis' sake and never intentionally to misrepresent.

One sunny morning Mildred and I called on a couple like ourselves who were once wrapped up in the hen business. As we sat in their pleasant kitchen reminiscing about this and that, we got to talking about raccoons. I don't know why it is, but any time farmers who have raised any corn at all get together the subject of these little masked bandits is apt to arise.

"Do you have trouble with coons now?" I asked.

"No," my friend replied. "We declared war on them a while back and since then we haven't been troubled. They used to get into my henhouses, and the game warden came down and we had a consultation. We decided a box trap was the thing to use. So I built one according to the proper plans and set it, but I had no luck. I found the coons were smart enough when they walked in after the bait to keep their back humped up so the trap wouldn't lock shut. And when they'd cleaned up the bait, they would back out, no worse for their trouble."

He continued. "I told the game warden about my problem, so he furnished me with some steel traps. Now I put one in a barrel and neatly arranged some garbage around it so it wouldn't be noticed, and I ran the trap chain out of the barrel and nailed it to the floor.

"Now, I'd set the thing on the end of my porch, and that night my dog began to bark. I looked out. And would you believe it? That raccoon reached down and pulled up the chain, sprung the trap, threw it out on the porch, and then proceeded to eat whatever he wanted to out of the barrel!

"Well, the next day I drilled a hole in the bottom of the barrel and ran the chain up from underneath. That night the moon was still good and bright and when my dog began to carry on, I got up and looked out the window again. The coon was perched on the top of the barrel and he was reaching down very carefully when all of a sudden there was a great snap and he was caught. He let out a yelp. Another great coon came running along, opened up my tool box, took out my wrecking bar, climbed up into the barrel and pried his friend loose."

About this time Mildred seemed to think that perhaps this was a little out of the ordinary and, after some prodding, he confessed it was.

But then he said, "You know, those critters are awfully smart. I had some pigs up across the road. I liked to mix up the slop for them the night before so I could feed them quick in the morning and get off to work. Well, these raccoons got to turning the button on the hog house door so that by morning there wasn't much left for the hogs.

"I decided something had to be done. So I arranged three traps around that slop pail and I was sure it would be impossible not to catch them. However, the next morning all three traps were sprung, the slop pail was nearly empty, and there weren't a coon in sight.

"So, the next night I re-arranged those traps. And would you believe it? I caught one coon in all three!"

The time had come for coffee to be passed around and by that time the subject of box traps came up again.

My friend continued, "I built two or three extra-large-size box traps to take care of the coons that were getting into my henhouse. I must confess I caught more skunks than coons. I used to take them to the river, tip the boxes up and the skunks would slide right out into the water. They didn't seem to mind getting wet some as they swam to the farther shore.

"Well, I was telling a friend of mine about all the skunks I was transporting from the farm and he came up with the idea that a fellow he knew who had been plaguing him some ought to be taught a lesson. So, one morning he borrowed one of these skunks and put him into the trunk of this fellow's car. I says, "he'll starve, won't he?"

He said, "No, he's kind of sloppy and the trunk is full of popcorn and old apple cores. The skunk could last at least three days."

My friend continued. "The truth was the skunk didn't have to worry for that very night this fellow gathered up some of his friends and headed over into Vermont to a local gin mill. They got tanked up pretty good and on the way home they made such an infernal racket they disturbed the skunk beyond the limit of his patience, and he let go a mighty charge. So they tell me, the car pulled over to the side of the road, all four doors opened at once, and the occupants tumbled out. The car's owner threw open the trunk and out ambled the skunk just as proud as you please and headed into the woods.

"But even though we caught a lot of skunks, we eventually cleaned out the coons," he concluded.

The time to leave had come. It had been a pleasant visit and we left with adequate instructions as to how to build a proper box trap for raccoons. Now all I have to do is to build one and see what luck I have. In any case, after I get it set I'll keep my tool box under lock and key.

Beaver Pond

AS EACH SUMMER DAY draws to a close, near to the hour when the bullfrogs begin to "sing-out" their evening hymns of "Ga-rumps," I once again travel to our beaver pond.

Some of the shouting frogs may be just plain braggarts who had gained a territorial claim. Other frog voices may have been raised for the purpose of loudly expressing their presumed ability to secure a claim.

After awhile the frogs ceased blaring out their societal position and a sort of silence reigned. The near quiet allowed the victors to better hear the moans of the vanquished. Whatever the case, following the period of disquiet, the evening was near silenced.

For a time I sat and watched the lengthening shadows push the silver sun-sheen off the meadow grasses eastward of the pond. I was anxiously waiting the arrival of our recent beaver visitor. We have not had beavers in the pond for several years and thus no repair work was done on the dam. The pond size had diminished considerably, that is until this beaver arrived a couple of months back. I know not what it's gender is, but suspect it is a young male that has wandered from the Ashuelot River seeking a place of his own. Correct or not, I granted it masculinity.

Suddenly, without a ripple, the animal's nose and face appeared close to the shore. Our "new" Mr. Beaver had learned that at near dusk, he would find a table of apples set before him.

During the waning days of July, I began these evening visits for I had not wished to disturb the animal at work.

It was now apparent from this beaver's progress that working on the old broken dam had occupied most of his waking moments. He had recreated a fully mature pond.

My first visit was to the north end of pond and my stay was just long enough to leave several apples. Mr. Beaver quickly learned that following my early evening visitations, apples appeared floating in his water.

As I continued my visits, he freely accepted my contributions as an evening treat. While I watched, he ate them without any objection. Truth to tell, those evening visits have really become my "treat."

On one particular evening it appeared that a hatch of some water-born insect was rising to the surface of the pond. Single dragonflies stopped in their flight momentarily to break the water surface and harvest a newly hatched bug of some sort. While the single dragonflies were dimpling the surface at their feeding, pairs of dragonflies chased each other, zigzagging around and across the smooth, open water. Was theirs a territorial dispute or were they engaged in a mating ritual? Knowing very little about the habits of these interesting insects, I can't answer my own question.

While watching the dragonflies or damselflies (it is hard for me to tell the difference), I was reminded that years ago, I really enjoyed working a featherweight fly rod over an unruffled pond. (I also was nimble enough to check a hatch rising to the surface.) During the search through my dry fly collection, I usually found one that was a close duplicate of the hatching insect. Experience had taught that such a fly would often tempt a trout to rise and the fun would begin.

The Old Barn

ONCE I WATCHED an October sky at sunset. It was not long before discovering it had shouldered the color tones of our flaming hillside's brilliance. The sky borrowed red and orange, and from them created lengthy streaks of brightness that were used to usher the evening heavens along their way.

My gaze dropped from the sky. I watched the hillside, half expecting to see the flaunting of its colors had moderated. How beautifully brilliant they still were! Apparently the sky had used such stealth in its borrowing that the hillside had not become aware of any tampering.

I was saddened by the thought that all too soon, like the fresh colors of the evening sky, the brilliance of the leaves of flame would diminish more swiftly than I would wish. Apparently the sky had used such stealth in its borrowing that the hillside had not become aware of any tampering.

✺

I recall an old fashioned winter day's walk. Travelling a country road, I passed by a barn whose promise of ever being useful, as measured by man's sense of worth, had long passed. From its eaves, snow hung in a forelock and made a ragged edge. Of the great twin doors, one was partly open, the other thrown back against the barn and held by snow. A smaller door stood to its left, splayed outward

65

hung by one hinge, and held by snow. It appeared the last productive toiler of the soil had long since departed.

I wondered who's left to know what this barn had been to the folks who had earned their living here. Someone could tell me, but I doubt finding them would be easy. If I ever did though, I'd ask, "Who owned this place?"

After a name had been offered, I'd half expect the inquired of to add: "The barn owned them!"

I suppose, as a matter of fact, they really owned each other—the man his hands and back, the barn its shelter for the stock. Twice a day the barn would call the farmer forth to feed and milk his cows. Call him at early morn from across the road where he himself had bedded down. Call him from his warm home and force him out, well before the day had broke.

In winter, through driving, deepening snows, his lantern pushed a yellow circle of light before him. He'd hold tight to the lantern bail with hand outstretched and with the other try to hide his face from a lacerating wind. And when he'd made the barn he'd kick away the snow before the smaller door, lift up the latch his father'd made and tug it toward him.

The opening door pushed the snow before it and piled it so's to keep it from opening too far back. The farmer used just force enough to edge himself into the barn and then slam-shut the door. The biting wind no longer scarred his face. He found the cold had already gotten in though. When he opened the inner stable door, warmth there was to greet him. It came at him, heady with the scent of cattle. He didn't mind the smell. He'd said so many times. But, when his wife suggested his barn boots be left in the shed outside the kitchen door, he obliged.

The animals heard him stomping snow from his boots. As the lantern light burst through the inner door, the stanchions rattled as the cattle stretched the night from their bones. They anticipated grain and hay would soon be fed. He hung his lantern behind the cows on a hook he'd made from baler wire. It was fashioned strong and put high enough so's nothing could reach it and send it crashing down to set the place afire. The cattle and the barn were his "tomorrow." Both had to be well protected.

In truth, the stock and barn were his future, a fact he'd learn to accept. Without them, he thought, he'd lose his independence. Occasionally though, he did cogitate about whether he believed that was so or not. And, as the thought meandered through his mind, he speculated as to which his master really was. The barn, or the livestock? Perhaps, but even so, if he had his druthers, he'd rather have them than be like his neighbor down the road who worked for other men. With his barn, he worked for himself. When he got right down to it, he knew the barn and he served each other.

I walked on. The weak, winter sun warmed my back as I traveled the road. The fields the other side of the wall from me were smooth and shiny white. They ran down to a brook, long since silenced by winter's cold. I wished I might hear it speak. Ice covered it and silenced what water words there were. Snow covered the reeds and grasses along its banks, so gave no shade to lurking trout. That would come with spring. For now, I'd have to be satisfied with the squeak of snow beneath my boots.

I thought I saw a movement within the crevasses of the wall. Stopping, I saw nor heard nothing. Quiet overwhelmed, except in my mind where thoughts about the barn still echoed. I turned around to look once more at the simple, abandoned structure. No doubt raised with the help of neighbors, a year or two perhaps before "the first shot was heard around the world." I'm sure an adze was swung by neighborly hands to hew the beams and work at the mortising and tenoning. Ropes were used to raise it, that and a jug of cider.

I have never been able to look at old structures without thinking about the folks who built them and later used them. I suppose that's because my ancestors came early to New England; Ward, on my mother's side in 1638, Cole, on my father's side in 1635. According to "General Artemas Ward, a Study," published by a the Ward

Museum in Shrewsbury, Mass., supported by Harvard University, the Continental Congress appointed General Ward, (my great-plus grandfather) as second in command of the revolutionary forces under George Washington.

Would that our forefather's spirit of freedom be etched in our hearts and actions, this day and all the days to come.

October Sky

ONCE I WATCHED a late October sky at sunset and saw it shoulder the color tones of our declining hillside brilliance.

It borrowed red and orange and created lengthy streaks of brightness, and used them to usher the evening heaven along its way. My eyes dropped from the sky, looked at the hillside and saw that it was still flaunting its colors. How beautiful they were! Apparently the sky had used such stealth in its taking that the hillside had not noticed. I was saddened by the thought that all too soon, like the new colors of the evening sky, the leaves of flame would fade faster than I wished.

The freshly painted western sky gradually changed. It had deliberately advanced from bright blue and now was passing through all its color cycles toward the cool darkness of day's end. Dark blues, a basic possession of the sky even during daylight, all too soon overwhelmed the brighter hues. I watched as red and orange shades drifted and melded clandestinely into purple and the purple into black. A metamorphosis that should have been unhurried moved all too swiftly.

During those moments while the reddish-purple hues stained the sky my thoughts transported me to a time just a few days before. It was on a late afternoon, while picking our fall raspberries, that purple as a color had become important to me. I like picking raspberries, the fruit that Henry David Thoreau spoke of as being, " . . . the most innocent and Simple of fruits, the purest and most ethereal."

The Sun Soothed the Sea

Life is a miracle. Life is beautiful, bright, happy. It is also dark, dreary and disappointing. I can take the disappointments and not dwell on them. I school myself not to remember them when all is excitingly, wonderfully alive. It takes the one to balance the other. To balance death it takes life. So life is a circle, a beginning and an ending all at the same time. And Nature displays it so. Perhaps to you it is the circle of day and night, perhaps the turning of the four seasons. But to me it is the sun and rain, the land and water. All the same, it is the circle of life that I wrote about when I wrote "The Sun Soothed the Sea." But there was one other ingredient—*love*. These words were penned with love.

THE SUN SOOTHED THE SEA, captured some of it, gathered it into clouds, and made it ready for the wind to push far over the land and there to fall—and there to fall.

And tumbling, it became a mountain stream rushing back toward the sea. It fumbled for the place of spilling over. Rushing down the glen, buffeted by a rocky bed, churning, roiling, smoothing to a calm rounded edge, then spilling o'er a fall and smashing to a pool below. It was water drapery woven by sun rays—a fabric holding tiny mirrors reflecting a torrent of color. Each splash of falling water became as sparkling gems—ruby, emerald, and turquoise. Whatever jewel man's eye can hold, and as many as he could wish, filled the glen with a precious mist.

Tiny sprays of water carried by the wind rest upon a cheek like an elfin tear.

The torrent below the falls rushed on until it tired of rushing. And when it reached the valley floor it seemed to move not at all, not even enough to cause a water reed to nod. Only a rippling wind could stir the mood, yet still it flowed slowly on toward the sea.

ℜ➡

Breaking waves at the edge of the rolling sea crashed against the craggy headland and became a thousand twisting, glistening, falling pieces. The land was a wizard and the sea was transformed into a treasury of color plumes.

The sea roared in agony.

Firm and powerful, each swell advanced only to be sundered by the land. Seething and frothing with discontent, each fractured splint furtively slid over the tormenting rocks to once more compose a conspiracy against its adversary.

But the land was unmoved.

Still, the land admired the violence and fury of the sea. It respected its majesty. Although unconquered, it permitted the monarch to retain dignity in defeat.

Sailing, crying, watching from unseen hammocks in the sky, the sea gulls accepted the battle as one that would always be without victory. Even when the dark green swells shatter into clouds of snow and cover the headland for a time, the gulls know black rocks will shine again. They wheel and drift and with wanton voices try to pierce the shout below. Theirs is but a sharp shaft, a momentary sting, that leaves no mark on the echo of the sea's lament.

The sun soothed the sea, capturing some, gathering it into clouds and making it ready for the wind to push far over the land and there to fall—and there to fall.

The Magic of the Fireplace

I'M NOT SO SURE BUT THAT a fireplace is more a state of mind than a physical thing. True, it contributes warmth to the body but it also contributes warmth to the soul.

When a winter day's chores are done, I like to sit before an open fire. It becomes a haven for my mind. With golden tongues of flame licking at the blackened bricks as they reach for the chimney flue, a thing of magic comes to pass. Imagined images form that sometimes take me back in time and sometimes catch me up and fly me far into the future to that mysterious province of desire, a Shangri-La of my own. But whichever way the flames transport me I grant it to be a pleasant pilgrimage. We have to grab at pleasantness and hold it tight, for too often our whirling world is too real for dreaming.

When the flames die to red-hot coals and I have not had enough of firelight fantasy, I add a stick or two of oak or maple or birch or whatever is left in the wood box that will bear me along for an hour more. And while the final logs are being devoured I feel my spirit, worn thin by the work of the day, begin a quiet return.

Like the dreams of sleep, the dreams of wake do not long linger in the conscious mind. Now and then, though, we recall them and a cherished moment lives again. It is something like the things we see that others do not, the way we feel and are alone in the sensation. When I look at a meadow in summer, I see ripe timothy heads drooping and sunlight glancing off green grass blades that are not green at all but sheened with silver. And so I see only what appears. When the grass whispers to the wind I hear it, but it matters not what its communication—that is between the wind and the grass. It is no affair of mine.

Once, I placed a birch log over red coals and watched white bark char brown, then blacken. Light smoke rose, darkened, then burst into a yellow flame. The tattered bark curled, caught fire and began to burn. Flames gnawed the wood with flashing teeth. Abruptly, it was a late fall day and I was back at the woodland's edge where the birch had grown. I had cut it down because it leaned too far into the field.

As I worked the birch tree into fire-log lengths, I heard a wiry chatter. Some birds were near. I half expected chickadees who were wont to share some thoughts with me whenever we found ourselves together, for pausing to pass the time of day had become a custom with us. (We never settled important matters of state, always just a pleasant conversation.) These birds, though, offered a new dialogue. I couldn't clearly make them out for their voices from a hemlock top were muffled.

Looking in their direction, I spied a movement. These visitors were smaller than chickadees—gray mites of birds. As the sun was more behind than beside them, I could not call them by name. I pondered. Smaller than chickadees, warblers perhaps? Too late in fall for most of those. These birds seemed smaller than warblers. Kinglets came to mind. One disclosed a golden splash when the sun struck its head as it made a quick dash to a leafless limb. Without speaking, it had been announced, a golden-crowned kinglet.

What a fitting name for this regal mite! And as the others of the flock joined it, I watched their heads as closely as I could, looking for a flash of scarlet. On another occasion I had seen a ruby-crowned kinglet mingling with a small flock of golden-crowned. How lovely to see them together! Having a visit from kinglets is a gentle experience. Although these birds are rather flighty—a bit nervous, you might say—they really don't appear to be afraid. I've never known them to linger long anywhere. They act like rest is for old folks while their business is motion. I am exhilarated by them.

When the birch log was nearly spent and the kinglets had faded with the flames, I tossed a piece of split maple on the coals and, sitting back, noticed that one edge was worn, polished somehow. And then I remembered, it was part of a hollowed bole that many feet had polished smooth. The maple had been a den tree that had fallen before a summer storm. When bucking it up, I found in a section of the upper trunk a bole where many kinds of wild things had established sanctuary. But I had been surprised when I'd got it split for there were few clues as to who had resided there last. A half-chewed acorn with cap attached and some tattered bark was all. Although the hollowed-out place had been large enough to house a raccoon or great horned owl, it may have been that nothing had nested there. It may have been only a temporary shelter from an untamed storm.

Eh? What's that—clock striking eleven? Can't be!

Well, it's time to head for bed.

As I poke the fire for the last time and place a screen before it, it comes to me—I have not only warmed the outer man but the inner man as well.

A fireplace is, indeed, a magical thing.

Winter Approaches

ALL TOO SOON winter winds will force black branches to propel their shadows across cool, sunlit places. Looking out my window this December day, only an isolated few of once fall-brilliant leaves cling stubbornly to tree skeletons. They are the few, death-darkened leaves that assisted in the creation of bright colored landscapes but weeks ago. Today, rain-washed and dull brown, they cling tightly with a close-fisted grip. Some will hold into spring when new leaf growth will shoulder them unceremoniously to the ground.

As December skies darken, the flakes of swirling snow will drift downward from a gray sky and the voice of the wind will be sharp. When the skies lighten again, the wind will become gentle, quiet will set in, and a hushed New Hampshire will be readied for winter.

Nature is Not Always Serene.

AS I SAT IN A PATCH OF SUNLIGHT one winter day on an old leather-seated chair that Grandfather once prized, and looked toward the mountain, I was startled to see a gray shroud slowly come between me and the mountain. The cloud-smoke smoldered, grew darker and shut me out. A winter storm was coming up.

My mind ran back in time to a winter's day when I'd sat and looked out the window of Grandfather's house toward a far hill. A storm had struck the night before and the trees were heavy with snow. The whole hillside was painted white with just enough of black tree trunks and branches showing to make an etching. That morning, the early sun made the snow spark like sparklers on the Fourth of July.

Then a cloud of silver rose from the hillside, spun across the hill face and swirled down into the valley out of sight. The wind had risen. It often does the morning after a storm. Good thing, too, for it lightens the burden of the trees and keeps them from being forever bent. (Though 'tis ice that's more than likely to bend the trees and keep them bowed down like they were in a perpetual state of prayer. Yes, I hate to see the afterwards of an ice storm for the damage it can cause.)

Two crows, that morning, started from a meadow below and headed for the shelter of the snow-clad pines. I watched them. Try as they might, they couldn't keep together. The wind ordered one here and tossed one there. They were as helpless as two dried oak leaves tossed in the wind. But, finally they reached the pines and a safe haven. I've always liked crows, admired them really, and I was truly glad for them that day.

Strange, nearly sixty years have passed since then, yet it all comes back so clear.

The storm struck as darkness fell. Grandfather, the hired man and I were in the barn. I'd finished my chore of feeding the calf. The storm rattled the windows and made the great door groan. When chores were done, we trudged toward the house. Even with my head bent low, the snow stung my face and made me squint my eyes near shut. The storm screamed like a locomotive running to escape the dark of midnight.

During supper we paid the storm no mind, but afterwards, sitting before the fire and concentrating on a game of dominoes, it intruded upon our thoughts. I became apprehensive when long branches of the old elm scraped against the house. And when they fingered the window panes, I was sure a ghost had entered my upstairs bed chamber. I was equally certain I didn't want to disturb it. I reasoned that if there was a ghost up there, let him be. I could camp down on the front-room sofa and make out just fine.

I tried to concentrate again on the game of "double-nines." The game was over all too soon. I was about to bring up the subject of sleeping downstairs when Grandfather rose from his chair and spoke. "Time to climb the golden stairs," he said.

Hesitatingly, I mentioned my plan. The clock struck nine. Grandfather opened the clock case door, took the silvered key in hand and wound it full. He often didn't answer right away. "All right," he said, "I'll help you make up a bed." Later, as he headed up the stairs he said, "Sleep tight! Don't let the bedbugs bite!"

That night was a long one, but the day broke fine.

A Woods Walk after a Storm

AFTER A WINTER'S SNOW, I like to look out our north window to watch fresh winds free black branches and dark green conifers from the cover of their new blanket. After the woods have been near-swept clean, the landscape no longer has that softened, gossamer look. Instead, the behavior of the wind has served somewhat to darken the day. But not my spirit.

Swirling swarms of drifting snow sift through the open woods and fall to the forest floor. The snow covers any evidence that wild things may have trespassed there. Some snow drifts like clouds of ocean spume across our fields. Snow-smoke is hurled against age-bent weed stalks and they are painted white.

As I watch the winter winds at work, I see blue jays poking at dried fruit in the swaying tops of our old apple trees. Suddenly, something there is that tugs at me and I can no longer remain within the warm walls of our two-hundred-year-old farm house. I am impelled by some mysterious urge to bundle up and join the day from without.

As I pass beneath the apple trees, I wonder who it was that planted them. Other than their growing less refined, they have looked the same to me for the past fifty years. I'll attribute the planting to "old settlers" who farmed this place long before my time. It must be now an age ago. Old apple trees are, indeed, true treasures and especially so for wild creatures. So, too, they were to James Whitcomb Riley when he wrote his delightful poem, "The Orchard Lands of Long Ago." He devised his first stanza thus:

The orchard lands of Long Ago!
O drowsy winds, awake, and blow
The snowy blossoms back to me.
And all the buds that used to be!
Blow back along the grassy ways
Of truant feet, and lift the haze
Of happy summer from the trees
That trail their tresses in the seas
Of grain that float and overflow
The orchard lands of Long Ago!

ॐ

Although it had appeared so, as I entered the woods I soon found that the winds had not released all the snow from the trees. Some was left as a surprise for me. Fine flakes drifted between my collar and neck and cooled me down a trifle but not enough to drive me back to inside civilization. At least not yet.

I followed a path that I knew well. Perhaps it was made at the time of the planting of the apple trees. That farmer may have used it in getting out his winter's wood. Although 'tis more likely that this was once a tote road constructed to allow old growth pine to be harvested. Some of it frames our house that, as far as we can tell, was built two centuries ago.

I mused upon these old settlers as I walked, and before long I half expected to meet a man walking toward me. I assumed that he would also be strolling about the woods as was I, without any particular purpose. I also conjectured that, as was the custom of that day, beneath his great coat he would be fashionably dressed in homespun clothing made of flax and wool, consisting of a ruffled shirt, short breeches and long stockings. I imagined that he would be sporting knee buckles, a powdered wig and a cocked hat.

However, it was much more likely that if I did come upon someone traveling the woods, it would be a man dressed much less ostentatiously and he well could be walking beside his ox team as they skidded out logs together. The sale of timber, then as now, gave the means to landholders for paying taxes and purchasing necessary supplies for the family. But such a man was not abroad and I was disappointed that we could not have passed the time of day. I'd like to have known first hand of his family and what he had been up to and how his crops had been that year. But I remained alone in the woods. Well, not really so, for the chatter of a gray squirrel came through to me and, a moment later, the single call of a distant crow. Then the woods became quiet except for my footfalls. They bespoke of hardwood leaves beneath the snow, a sort of crunch that said, "Hello."

I approached the brook and it laughed softly. Not so much to itself, I thought, but to the whole woods. It voiced a cheery bubbling sound. Yes, it was doing more than conversing with the stones over which it flowed. Perhaps it might have been sending a whispered message to the sleeping trilliums that lined its edge. They would have to wait until spring to receive it. Here in the deep woods, May would be nearly in full dress before they would waken and bloom once again. The seasons, though, were already on the move, for a fringe of ice was reaching out from both banks. Not many more days would pass before the ice fingers would entwine with one another and still the brook.

I found a boulder bereft of snow and sat upon it. I looked up the path and wondered if, in fact, had there been an early settler coming toward me, lightly touching up his oxen with a goad, would there have been a Christmas spruce tied carefully upon his load? Or would my well-dressed stranger in powdered wig and cocked hat be dragging one behind? Yes, I wondered.

Grandmother's Christmas Tree

IN WINTER EVENINGS after darkness has settled into our valley and the bustle of the day has ceased, I like to spend some quiet moments sitting before the big kitchen fireplace. How pleasant it is to watch the bluish, white-tipped flames curl upward from under a good-sized rock maple log to join the yellow-orange blaze from the soft wood kindling. The faint wisps of wood smoke that have spilled surreptitiously into the room lend a delicate tang to the evening air.

Mesmerized by the flames and their crackling sounds, my mind frequently wanders to days gone by. And, when Christmas eve is with us, reminiscences of going to Oak Hill with my Grandfather Cole in search of "a Christmas tree for Grandmother" frequently have come to mind.

I did so enjoy going to the hill when it was just "Gramp" and me. He was a spare and energetic man, constantly busy, and when we went to Oak Hill he seemed always to be in a particular hurry. He couldn't wait to begin whatever things that continually needed doing. In spring, it was the pasture fence that needed fixing. In summer, stray cattle had to be looked for—those that had found a weak place in the fence or hadn't shown up with the others at Sunday morning salting time. In fall, after a heavy wind storm, we hastily perambulated the fence line to make any needed repairs. Gramp's attitude was different though, when we went after Grandmother's

Christmas tree. He wanted to please her and gave no appearance of caring how long it might take.

My mind drifts back into those long-ago days. I remember my grandfather as a most unusual man. He could call by name all of the trees and wildflowers beside our path and the animals that scurried across it. He could tell when it was going to storm and when it would be clear. He could tell what bird was singing and where it might locate its nest. He knew when the hay was ready to make and when silage corn was ready to cut. He could fix broken things and make new things. I used to wonder how he knew so much and, truth to tell, I still do. It's hard to beat the old-timers when it comes to just plain knowing.

Oak Hill begins in the valley beside the river and rises until it becomes the height of land. Open pasture lay at its feet but the rest of the hill was timbered, mostly with white pine, hemlock, maple, ash and red oak. At the summit great oak trees stood. It was from these that the hill had gained its name.

Winter or summer, whenever we visited Oak Hill, Grandfather stopped at the pasture spring. The water, ice-cold even on the hottest summer's day, bubbled up and splashed its way through alder thickets on its way to the river.

Near the high ground was a wetland area where balsam and spruce trees grew. Climbing the hill, we'd pass beneath wild apple trees and see where deer had pawed the snow away to get at the frozen fruit. Grandfather used to point to things like where a partridge had roosted the night before. He'd show me the thorn apple trees where the birds had fed on red, dried apples. Now and again a rabbit would start from under a brush heap and pound over frozen ground in search of a safer hide. I especially enjoyed arriving at the railroad bed that bisected the hill. I liked to walk the ties and balance upon the rails. Both were removed years ago.

At the swampy area where the Christmas trees grew Grandfather always would say: "Pick out the one you think Grandmother would like, Boy." As I stood and searched with an eager but unacquainted eye, he was ready with a hint or two as to what to look for when selecting "Grandmother's tree." When the tree was finally selected Grandfather swung the axe. It bit heavily into the tree and it was soon down. How proud I was to help drag the tree. On the way back to the wagon we'd stop and gather princess pine and hemlock boughs for decorations around window boxes and to drape beside the front door.

A trip with Grandfather for the Christmas tree was an exhilarating adventure and one that has created marvelous memories.

Oak Hill is mine now. Today the open pasture is closed mostly by poplars and gray and white birch. Early harvested hardwoods begat sprouts that are now nearly full-grown and ready to be harvested. The spruce and balsam have disappeared from the upper wetlands. There is an occasional trace of a first-growth oak stump now hidden beneath a hardwood canopy. The pasture spring, though, can still be found—its sweet water, still a delight to the taste.

Dying fireplace embers and fading remembrances announce it is time to give the fire one last poke before locking up for the night.

On Christmas Eve

During the years of my life that I can recall, Christmas Eve has held great meaning for me. On Christmas Eve, I receive great pleasure from re-reading the biblical story of Jesus's birth. That testament became even more meaningful during our years of tending live-stock. My emotions are described in the following paragraphs.

THE WINTER SUN, paled by distant haze, splashed its spray of rays through leafless hardwoods and created a shadow tapestry on snow covered fields.

The rough wind of the afternoon had blown itself out and the air became stilled and cold. As the weak sun faded beyond our western hills the sky colored slightly. A begrudging hint of warmth perhaps? The light sulked while it languished.

Looking out my west window on this late December day I watched the darkness creep over our valley. This was the season when an early weariness settled into my bones. It did so gradually as does ground fog when it rises in our valley.

As my mind drifted back to those days gone by, suddenly the old grandfather's clock in the kitchen struck five. Here at the farm, the stroke of five in the evening was the historically announced hour for milking to commence. After milking the cattle would be bedded down for the night.

I remembered how time passed slowly before all the chores would be done and the hour for sleep could come. In winter, more than at any other time of the year, barn chores became dulled by their sameness. The deliberate daily routine that accompanied daylight shortened days brought on a weariness that seemed to cling as each day was brought to a close.

Unexpectedly, as I was mulling over those sometime dreary days of yore, it came to me. Tonight was Christmas Eve! My spirit brightened!

For those who choose to earn their daily bread by caring for animals, Christmas Eve will always hold a special meaning. I remembered now that during my years while working the farm, the usual weariness disappeared on the anniversary night of the Miracle of Jesus' birth. The commonplace matter of taking care of our stock was transformed into pleasant labor. Walking to the barn on that special night, the cares of the day became as light as a new-fallen snowflake. Love for each other and our animals grew stronger.

How nice it would be, I thought, to leave the world behind for awhile and be escorted back to that wondrous night when Christ was born.

I have always loved those words from the gospel according to St. Luke: "And she brought forth her first-born son and wrapped him in swaddling clothes, and laid him in the manger; for there was no room in the inn." Those precious words still ring through my mind as clear as silver bells!

On Christmas Eve I have often wished I could have been one of the shepherds "abiding in a field, watching over their flock at night," when the Angel of the Lord appeared. The shepherds were "sore afraid" and I have no doubt I would have been also.

After milking was done and the cattle and sheep were fed, I enjoyed pausing for a while in our stable before returning to the house. Sitting on a bale of hay with my back against the wall of the sheep pen, I enjoyed listening to the sounds in the darkened barn. The stanchions creaked and groaned as the cows stretched their necks for an out-of-reach wisp of hay. The sheep made soft sounds as they selected a place to bed down in their straw. In a little while, after all the animals had laid down to rest, except for the near-whisper of their chewing, quiet set in.

In the hayloft above the stable it was not unusual to hear the kittens pouncing about, being not quite through with their play. In a little while, though, even they curled up in a snug nest of hay and fell fast asleep. Peace had arrived in the sleeping stable.

Leaving the warmth of the stable, I closed the barn door and immediately felt a magic in the air. This night is one that will draw families closer together. And somewhere, old friends will join to celebrate our Savior's birth. Threads of conversations will be pulled from a pattern of woven memories. Joy will abound, nurtured by the spirit of Christmas. And in the East, the star will shine.

It is my hope that the day will soon arrive when the people of the world will find in their hearts a love for one another and strive to work together to create a true and lasting peace on earth.

The Mountain

THERE MUST BE SOME unseen catalyst, mixed with sun and sky, that produces the magnetic force that draws me to the mountain. "Familiarity breeds contempt," they say. This may be so in some cases, but not for me where the mountain called Monadnock is concerned.

As I look back over the years, the mountain has always been mysterious and magical to me. Perhaps it may have been because of its size, for to a growing lad it loomed large indeed—as a giant against the eastern sky.

I believe I was fourteen the first time I climbed it. I still cherish the thrill of standing on the summit and being able to see "clear to Boston Harbor," or so I was told. I went up with my grandfather, my mother's father. It was his thirty-third ascent. I could hardly believe anyone could be that old and still be climbing mountains.

In the years since, my travels have taken me from my beloved New Hampshire to places where truly giant mountains abide. But always there has been a nagging longing, a compulsion to be back home where I could look at the Mountain. For that's what we have always called it—The Mountain. It is truly magnificent, an ever-changing thing of beauty as each day and each season unfolds. One can never become bored with it. The mountain is never ominous even when the blackness of a summer storm brings down the sky.

Its profile differs with one's vantage point. I like the view with my back to the west. It is from there I find Monadnock best, although I could not quarrel with one who chose a different view.

Grand Monadnock is better seen than described. If I were to attempt to describe it, I would be telling more of myself than of the mountain, for a description, of necessity, reflects the senses of the viewer. I don't believe it is possible to look at Monadnock and not to feel—to see and not to sense. One would have to be callous, indeed, not to be moved by its singular beauty.

Not only do I see The Mountain, but I sense its mood. Or is it a reflection of my own mood? And I note the scent of the air and hear the wind no matter how softly it moves the trees or pushes the clouds. If it is spring, I catch the scent of damp places, and on shady knolls the sweet perfume of the delicate trailing arbutus called mayflower. I smell the dead leaves, too, and other fragrances. The warm time of spring has a "savor," as the summer and fall have their savor. And even the white sterility of winter has its essence—cold, stinging snow.

But I must tell of twisting grasses, of mossy places, gnarled shrubs, and of other things on The Mountain not so much noticed. It is these little things that make the whole Mountain. The scratching in dry leaves of the towhee and fox sparrow. The noisy flicker's call. The plaintive whistle of a chickadee. The bubbling song of the purple finch. All are a part of The Mountain.

When the amethystine shadows clothe the base of The Mountain and the sun caresses the summit with a golden light—then, too soon, the night will descend. Now comes the time of hoot owls, barred and great horned. The partridge ceases to drum in the lowlands, and on the hillsides the twittering flight calls of the woodcock speak of evening.

Another day in the life of man draws to a close. A twinkling of eternity has passed for The Mountain.

Other than Earthbound

IN CHILDHOOD everything seems possible—if not today, then someday. I guess that's when I first became acquainted with "someday." I've always looked forward to arriving there. Perhaps, one day, I shall. Oftentimes, though, I have discovered there is more joy in anticipation than in the granting of a dream.

Long ago during an early-spring day that was full of rain, I huddled beside a gray boulder beneath a red oak tree that still clung to its last year's leaves. I watched a drop of rain fall on a leaf, gather itself, then fall again. The diminutive droplet journeyed downward from leaf to leaf until it reached the ground, then slowly disappeared. Later, it would nurture the grasses and the wildflowers.

I especially enjoy creatures who are not earthbound—flying things, especially birds. And, long ago, I learned that I, too, could be other than earthbound. It simply appeared so. Indeed, I found I could soar as high as the farthest cloud and beyond, to where each cloud disappeared. For wings—my imagination.

How fortunate we are who live in New Hampshire. What beauty we share! It takes no special eye or learned mind to appreciate what we have here.

New Hampshire has been good to me and good for me. Here it has been that I have feasted upon the marrow of life.